GW00481854

Aidee

"...produce the chocolate first!"

BALLYHAY BOOKS

Published by Ballyhay Books,
an imprint of Laurel Cottage Ltd.
Donaghadee, N. Ireland 2006.
Copyrights Reserved.
© Text by Aideen D'Arcy 2006.
All rights reserved.
No part of this book may be reproduced or
stored on any media without the express written
permission of the publishers.
Printed by Gutenberg Press, Malta.

ISBN 1 900935 56 2

To my Mum and Dad,

…who called me by my name and ran,
And faded through the brightening air.

They weighed so lightly what they gave.

W B Yeats

---- ∽ ----

Acknowledgements

---- ∽ ----

I'd like to thank Etta Cowman of the Local History Department, Waterford City Council Library Services, for answering my queries about the Waterford Coat of Arms and the wreck of the *Alfred D. Snow*.

When I rang to make the initial enquiry I found myself speaking to a really friendly assistant who showed a lively interest in my book. Niamh Baldwin turned out to be a grand-daughter of Cissie, wife of my dad's best friend in his youth, with whom I subsequently enjoyed a fascinating conversation and shared a few memories. Warm thanks to you both.

And thanks always to Issy, who, though coming late to Dungannon, loves it almost as much as I do.

Contents

Prologue

"You've left out all the best stories!"

That's what everyone told me after they had read *Lie Over Da*, and while I'm not about to get embroiled in that argument, I soon realised that there were indeed more tales demanding to be told, more people to celebrate. I hadn't quite cancelled my debt to the past. I suppose I never will.

The legacy of the marvellous people who enriched my world was in danger of being subsumed into the experiences that life throws at us, to be lost forever at the bottom of a pile of memories that we mean one day to excavate, but never get around to it. Writing is a kind of 'getting around to it'. As I stirred through the melting pot of my consciousness looking for details, there surfaced a whole host of things I had forgotten I knew, like how to read a person's character from the bumps on his head, or that certain people were said to have the ability to 'lift the spool of the breast' by applying a cup full of oatmeal to the breastbone and repeating the procedure until there was no longer an impression made in the mixture when it was taken away. The fact that I have absolutely no idea why anyone should want to do this, or what ailment it might be supposed to cure, diminishes not at all the fascination I felt as a youngster on hearing that someone was about to have this treatment carried out! Why should these memories be allowed to fade and die? They deserve better.

This book is an affectionate memoir of Dungannon, where I grew up, and Passage East, that lovely village on the Waterford coast where I spent many happy holidays, and where my dad was born. It's a celebration of the humour, wit, and essential goodness of the people I knew and loved, and always, and without overt intention, it's a testament to the personality of my mother. Maureen Campbell D'Arcy was a larger than life character. It's hard to keep her off the page, so I accept the inevitable, and let her have her say.

My three guardian angels – my mother, my Aunt Mona, and my Granny Campbell – taught me to love words and value people, and my dad, Patrick D'Arcy, gave me a love of the sea and respect for all humankind. They were themselves the greatest gift of all and I miss them. This book is also, therefore, a small stitch in the quilt of time that keeps our memories warm.

If you recognise yourself or someone dear to you in these tales, then know that they are told with love and recorded in an effort to preserve something of what life can take away but no amount of living can give us back – our heritage.

If you're not here in these pages, then maybe it's time you started to write down your own stories, before it's too late.

Long Faded Glories

John 'Hawkeye' Campbell

Quiet and love I sing –
The cairn on the mountain crest,
The cailin in her lover's arms,
The child at its mother's breast.

Beauty and peace I sing –
The fire on the open hearth,
The cailleach spinning at her wheel,
The plough in the broken earth.

Travail and pain I sing –
The bride on the childing bed,
The dark man labouring at his rhymes,
The ewe in the lambing shed…

No other life I sing –
For I am sprung of the stock
That broke the hilly land for bread,
And built the nest in the rock!

———— ❧ ————

Thus Joseph Campbell, in *I am the Mountainy Singer*, writing of the elements that made up his own particular world, the things that brought him pleasure and moulded him into the man he was, the poet he would become.

We are all shaped by our surroundings and the people we know, and if my acquaintances were of a very different hue from the ones Campbell commemorates, they were special too, and deserve to be applauded. Many of the people who enriched my childhood have passed along the road before me, but every day I find them knocking on the shutters of memory, demanding attention. Since I passed fifty, I find myself doing more and more of what my dear Uncle Wilf described so strikingly as a feature of growing older; *"You live backwards, you see, daughter, for when there's not much time to look forward to, what can you do but look back? And as you get older, and when you're not too fit, each day is like a year, you think when you get up in the morning you'll never see bedtime. But the years are like days, and when I remember something that happened to me when I was a young cub, sure it's only like yesterday."*

He was, as always, both wise and funny, and he was right.

I was born in 1954 in Birmingham, a place which means absolutely nothing to me, partly because I left it when I was six weeks old and did not set foot in it again for twelve years, and partly because my mother loathed it, and had no fond recollections of it to share with me. But I grew up in Dungannon, a mill and factory town with a rural hinterland, described by one anonymous commentator as *humpy Dungannon*. All its main streets radiated down from the Market Square, also known as 'The Diamond', which backed onto the Castle Hill, where the great O Neill clan had a fortification in earlier days. The other side of this arrangement was that if you lived, as we did, on the Donaghmore Road, all the roads radiated *up*. Another versifier sees it in somewhat more romantic terms as *'that old grey town, its tree-decked crown, Dungannon on the hill'*, but however you choose to look at it, it's my home town, and unlike Birmingham, it meant everything to me. To my mother, Maureen D'Arcy, the people were the heart of corn: warm, funny, and generous, open-handed with their time or their belongings, and always quick with a quip or a comment. The town in my childhood was a beautiful town, with fine buildings, well-stocked shops, bustling streets, only a mile or so away from a lush and verdant countryside. Let no one visiting the sad wraith of the town today judge it on what they see now. Thirty years of the Troubles, the decline of the linen industry, the demise of farming as a viable way of life, and of course, emigration, all took their toll on its prosperity, and what is left today is a mere shade of the town it used to be. But where else would you find a town with street names like The Rat's Pad, Babe's Entry, and Shammellane?

It was always a late town, with shops staying open until their owners felt like closing, and even then, if you really needed something, you only had to bang on a door, for most of the proprietors lived over or beside their premises. It's not the first time Dennis McNaney was knocked up at three in the morning to fill out a prescription that someone had forgotten to collect during normal hours, whatever they were! He was once questioned by an army patrol who observed him putting his bin out at about four a.m., but it was soon made clear to them that this was not unusual, and no doubt they grew accustomed to him repeating the procedure on many a subsequent occasion.

Dungannon had great shops: Watson & Bell's, with a postbox outside the front door to which local children were often dispatched with a letter and the instruction, "Away and throw that into Bell's hole"; Balance and Lennon's for hardware; The Milestone, selling excellent cooked meat and ham; chemists' shops like Reynolds's, Quinn's, and Kelly's; Joe Hayden's for fine furniture; McKinley's for fancy goods and a Christmas toy showroom to make any child's mouth water – and parent's heart quail; Magowan's for household goods; and a couple of fine dress shops – Alexander's, the old Menary's, Fox's, and a shop whose name I could never spell for I never saw it written down, but it was pronounced something like Goorwitches. I use 'pronounced' loosely. This is how it was pronounced by the locals, but whether that was its original pronunciation or not, who can say?

It had great shopkeepers too, who knew how to go for the hard sell. One of them was dealing with a hard-to-please customer who wanted to buy a coat, and had tried on nearly every one in the shop without making a selection. Finally, as he presented what was nearly the last of his stock the owner remarked,

"There now, that looks grand on you. Wouldn't it suit you great for going to Church?"

The customer frowned.

"I go to neither Mass, meeting, nor Church," he declared, not without a certain pride.

"Well now," returned the hard-pressed proprietor, "You'll not be ten minutes dead till you'll wish you had."

Many of the shops in The Diamond and elsewhere were long and slender with narrow entrances. This was an oddity of Dungannon and may have had its origins in the fact that the head-rents were based on the span of the frontage. Later on several shops would be amalgamated to give the wider fronts that I remember, but even in my time many shops were longer than they were broad. Alexander's was one of my favourites because whenever you purchased something, the assistant would put your money and payment details into a tubular receptacle and pop it into a glass-fronted box, whence it disappeared with a satisfying whoosh! After a few seconds, with a whirr and a rattle, back would come another tube with your change and receipt. Magic! I couldn't make up my mind whether I'd rather operate that apparatus or work in the Post Office, where I could get to use one of those sticky orange sponge pads which enabled you to count vast piles of notes in a twinkling. But the added attraction that some of the assistants in Alexander's had a pair of scissors tied by a cord to the belt of their blue shopcoats might have swung it in their favour.

Then there was Jack Quinn's, where you could buy any kind

of DIY equipment you needed, including sand and cement, and I well remember the day that Uncle Wilf carried a bag of sand from his shop to our house, a journey of about ten minutes; and before you say, so what? let me suggest you try to lift and hold, never mind carry, a bag of sand for even one! He would have been all right if no one had spoken to him, but this was Dungannon, and everyone he met wanted to stop and have a yarn. There was neither order nor organisation to Quinn's as far as the casual observer could see, but Jack or Arthur could find anything at the drop of a hammer. I remember going in to buy a gate catch. I watched in amazement as Jack climbed over a pile of boxes, removed another pile from a shelf, and after a moment exultantly produced the very thing I wanted. Needless to say, he didn't replace the boxes he had removed, so the pile on the floor grew larger and larger. That's probably why the only thing he didn't sell was a step-ladder.

There was Doran's for bicycles, and much else besides, Pagni's for the best chips outside of Italy, McCrystal's for toffee apples on the way home from school as Hallowe'en approached, and best of all, Mooney's in Irish Street, a tiny shop that on one side had shelves full of laundry waiting to be collected, and on the other a selection of small grocery items and cigarettes, but on the counter was a tiered display unit selling all manner of cheap and cheerful sweets, a child's delight and a dentist's nightmare. Parma violets that stained your lips purple, black jacks, sherbet fountains, flying saucers, cherry lips, acid drops, Lovehearts, Spangles, liquorice strips, white mice, spearmint pips, drumsticks. And in the jars behind the counter, jap desert, those little cubes of coconut coated in candy, pink, yellow, and brown; scented bon-bons that stuck to each other and to your teeth; birds' nests; rainbow drops; clove rock and brandy balls. I can taste them now. And who could forget the poor man who kept the brandy balls in a jar on the top shelf so that he had to get the steps to reach it down, or the day the four wee boys came into the shop to spend their pocket money? The first asked for a penn'orth of brandy balls, so the shopkeeper – it might have been John McGuckian, Mary Mooney's husband – toiled up the steps, brought down the jar, weighed out the sweets, made up a paper poke, and deposited the penny in the drawer, before restoring the jar to its rightful place. He turned to his next customer.

"What can I get you?"

"A penn'orth of brandy balls, please, sir."

So John repeated the sequence, dusted off his hands, leant across the counter, and fixed the third lad with a beady eye.

"What do you want, son?"

"A penn'orth of brandy balls, please."

Back he went, a sadder and wiser man, and this time before he replaced the jar he addressed the fourth cub.

"I suppose you want a penn'orth of brandy balls too?"

The child grinned toothily at him. "No thanks."

He settled the jar into place, descended the steps, folded them and put them away, before turning to the wee fellow.

"Now then, son, what is it you want?"

"A happ'orth of brandy balls, please sir."

The wonderful thing about Mooney's was that nothing on that display cost more than a penny, and often less. You could usually get two of something for that, and if you really wanted to eat on the cheap, you could get four sports, a kind of liquorice chew, for a penny, but I never sank as low as that. If you went in with sixpence, you came out with an armful of stuff. They had a wee home bakery in my mother's childhood, and Granny Campbell used to call in for a chat with Cissie Mooney when she was up the town. Whenever she had the child Wilfred with her, he would eye the buns and say, after a few moments, "Mama, I'm starving," and Cissie would always reply, "And maybe you could take a wee bun." Which he did. My grandmother spent weeks trying to break him of this habit for it mortified her, and finally it seemed as if she had succeeded. They had been inside the shop for about ten minutes without a word from Wilf; then:

"Mama?" She glared at him warningly. "What?" He grinned back.

"I'm not a bit hungry the day." Granny was speechless, Cissie in stitches. "Sure, maybe you could take a wee bun anyway, Wilfred son." Which he did.

I was used to people dropping in and out of our house as I grew up. My dad found it a big change from his own home in Passage East, where visitors were welcome as long as they were invited and you could plan for them, and nicknamed it 'Clapham Junction', but my mother considered it a poor day indeed if the door wasn't darkened on at least three occasions by the arrival of a neighbour or other visitor. It was not unusual for the Campbell family to be eating their dinner at nine o'clock at night, the day having been whittled away in making wee drops of tea for the innumerable callers who stepped in for a chat. It never occurred to anyone to refuse, and it never occurred to us not to join them! In the days when we had a range, my mother's good friend Veronica Rice, known as 'Gogga', would come in and pour herself a cupful from the teapot that always rested there, no matter how old or strong the brew it contained. Many a time my mother would say, "Och Veronica, you couldn't drink that! I made it hours ago. Put the kettle on and make a fresh drop." But she could, and did.

Before the new Girls' Intermediate School was built, our house on the Donaghmore Road looked over into Hales's Field. This was part of, really the remains of, a large estate, and in my mother's childhood there was a house on it occupied by a Miss Hale or Hales, the last of her family. She employed a gamekeeper to patrol her grounds with a shotgun over his shoulder, and well dare any youngster come within a hound's gowl of the wall, for he knew he'd be seen off with a sharp word and the threat of a pellet or two in a strategic place. Miss Hale had a reputation for meanness, as well as a standing order with a local butcher for a quarter pound of liver for her pet cat. One day she telephoned the butcher and instructed him in cut-glass tones: "Cancel the liver; Tiddles has caught a mouse."

———— ∞ ————

I remember a time when there were fewer cars on the road, a private telephone was a rare luxury but the phone boxes were never vandalised, and children actually wanted to go outside to play! The women of the street managed their houses and had time to stand at their front doors and chat, before the final flurry of activity which accompanied that hour of the day when the menfolk were expected home for tea. It was the era of a curious anomaly: on the one hand, your neighbours knew all about you; on the other, they left you alone. In every sense that mattered, they were there when you needed them. I cannot imagine a time in the Dungannon of my childhood when a man could lie dead in his house for weeks and no one miss him, yet it happens today with alarming frequency. In my own experience, I know of three men and one woman whose lives ended in this heart-breaking manner.

So, Joseph Campbell, who will I sing of? It might be The Hawk, otherwise known as Hawkeye or The Thin Man, for Dungannon was so fond of bestowing nicknames that one was rarely enough. He had lost an eye at a very early age and there were two versions of how it happened. The first was that as he was trying to wring a turkey's neck, the brute gave a flap of its wings and struck him in the eye, the resulting damage being such that it had to be removed. The turkey did not survive the encounter either, I believe. The second was that he was trying to undo a knot in his shoelace with a fork, and as he bent over the task, his arm jerked back and he stabbed himself in the eye; but I think this was a fabrication of my mother's, designed to keep me from doing anything that might require the application of mechanical assistance to an everyday job such as loosening knots. The stricture was unnecessary, because if I had been experiencing problems with my shoelaces, I would simply have slipped the shoes off, laces intact, as any sensible child would do, but she clearly didn't trust me. The only bit of the story I can vouch for is that The Hawk did indeed have a glass eye, and that my Grandmother Campbell

———— ∞ ————

was frequently sent for to help him put it in before he got so used to it that he could do it with his other eye shut.

He was tall and thin, attractive in his way with a certain air about him, and a manner of talking out of the side of his mouth that as a child I found fascinating. He wore his dark hair combed back from his forehead in that typical '50s style, and I recall him wearing a gabardine overcoat and a scarf. I thought him very stylish.

He disliked travelling in cars, and once got a lift home from some smart alec who, knowing of this aversion, thought it funny to sink the guttie all the way down the motorway, with the result that The Hawk was a bit shaky when he alighted in Dungannon. The driver addressed him in mock concern.

"What's the matter, John, was I driving too fast?"

"No," he drawled. "You were flying too low."

Charlie's pub in Irish street always hosted a lively discussion and one night the talk came round to films.

"What was the name of that film with Spencer Tracy, where he plays the fisherman who's after thon big fish?" asked someone. No one could remember. Most of the boys had seen it; my dad knew it was based on a novel by Hemmingway, but still the title escaped him. Some thought Tracy might have won an Oscar for it. Enter John.

"Hi, John! What was the name of that film where Spencer Tracy plays the man who's after the big fish?"

John, headed for his favourite seat at the back of the bar, shot back, without breaking stride, "The Johnny Owens Story."[1]

If you wanted to buy John a drink, he would ask for a De Kuyper's Gin. No wonder I thought him an exotic.

I might sing of Honest PG, darkly handsome, what the French call *distingué*, entrepreneur extraordinaire, who frequently turned

---

[1] If you're not from Dungannon, you'd need to be told that Johnny Owens was the wee man who came to Anne Street every week to sell fish, and whose cry of "Harnsla harns!" (Herrings Alive!) woke us many a morning. The film was *The Old Man and the Sea*.

up in our sitting room when he had had a few too many, there to sit a while till he gathered himself. My grandmother would find him there and he'd greet her with,

"It's only me, Mrs. Campbell. I'll be on my way shortly," and he would. He drove a Mercedes when most people rode bicycles, and many a wet morning I got a lift to school along with the dozen or so other kids who managed to pile in, in the days before safety regulations and seatbelts made such a thing impossible. He had a reputation as a bit of a daredevil, and lived up to it by being buried alive as a publicity stunt and driving a car across a frozen Black Lough. He met my Uncle Wilf one day and called him over.

"Here, boy! Is it true you did a wee job for Mick?"

"I did," says Wilf, curious. "Why?"

"Has he paid you yet?" Wilf laughed.

"Not yet." Mick was notoriously bad pay.

PG pulled out a roll of notes that would have choked a horse and waved them in front of my uncle.

"Here, then, take what you're owed; take a bit more for the delay. I'll make sure he pays me!"

Or it might be Kevin Close, bespectacled stalwart of the choir and the Musical Society, a man of stocky build and droll humour, dandering in to Kathleen's shop on a warm clammy evening in summer when there wasn't a breath.

"Hello, Kevin," my mother greeted him. "Isn't it close?"

"It is, Mrs. D'Arcy," he returned straight-faced. "And if they took the 'D' off your name, it wouldn't sound so hot either."

Or there's always The Crow, tiny in stature though big in heart, who would order a pint in Charlie's with the stipulation, "And push it well over on the bar." He and big Bob Grimes, six foot if he was an inch, enjoyed a running feud, and one day as the argument grew heated, The Crow snapped, "Quit spittin' up into my face."

It was Bob who told my mother that his niece had secured a good job in Belfast.

———— ⌘ ————

"She's a typewriter in an office," he explained. Around the same time he was describing a function he had been asked to assist with, complaining about the lack of the most basic facilities in the hall they were using.

"It was tarra," he said. "They had nothin'. We had to make do with an impoverished table."

And he refused point-blank to listen to a neighbour's complaints about the behaviour of his young nephews, saying, "Sure I can't be impossible for my brother's children."

Or Joe Comac who, concerned at the speed of change initiated by Vatican Two, remarked to a friend of mine,

"If you want to die a Catholic, you'd need to hurry up."

Or his wife Nellie, who, on being asked how she was feeling after a short illness replied,

"Not great. I went to open the front door the other day and I just dropped in two on the step."

Good men and true, every one of them. And the women weren't bad either!

As my mother grew older, she would sometimes look at her morning face in the mirror, clap her hands over her mouth in mock dismay and intone "the long faded glories," as she rolled her expressive eyes towards her reflection. She was quoting from *Let Erin Remember,* by the now largely forgotten balladeer and poet Thomas Moore, once the darling of the drawing-rooms of Regency England, a song that my Aunt Mona often sang in her sweet voice, accompanied by my mother's rich contralto. The Campbells all enjoyed a sing-song, and my mum also played the piano. Perhaps the gift of music was inherited from their aunt, Monica Campbell Doyle, who was entertaining her companions on the train from Belfast one day when still a young girl, when the door of the carriage opened to admit an elderly gentleman.

"Forgive me," he said with grave courtesy, "but you must allow me to shake the hand of the singer who has given us all such pleasure for the last few miles. It was a privilege to hear her."

Mona rarely sang for an audience, though old Mrs. Campbell

could always persuade her, that other Mrs. Campbell whose daughters, Una, Shona, and Susie, we were proud to number among our best friends. We visited each other's houses regularly when I was very young, and Susie always let me help with the preparations for supper.

"Aideen," she'd say, "I think it's time to get out the wee brown teapot."

This was a source of delight to me, for we used a metal teapot but Susie used a delph one, and I was mightily impressed by it. She it was who taught me to save any crumbs for the wild birds in winter, and she would lift me up so I could reach to throw the leftovers onto the top of the wee tin outhouse in the back yard for our feathered friends to pick at. Towards the end of their return visit to our house, Mrs. Campbell would say,

"And now Mona will give us *Maggie,*" and she would:

> *They say I am feeble with age, Maggie*
> *My steps are less sprightly than then;*
> *My face is a well-written page, Maggie,*
> *But time alone was the pen…*
> *They say we are aged and grey, Maggie,*
> *As spray by the white breakers flung,*
> *But to me you're as fair as you were, Maggie,*
> *When you and I were young.*

Mum was never afraid to ham up her voice for humorous ditties, though she could sing a tearjerker with the best of them. She told me that when she tried out for the Musical Society, its musical director, Fr. Austin Eustace, was delighted with her.

"Sopranos are ten a penny, Maureen," he said. "It's nice to get a good contralto. You'll be great in *Deep River.*" Whereupon her friend Danny McCrea piped up,

"Aye, up to the neck, Father."

She actually got more fun out of doing the make-up for the productions than singing in them. She was one of two girls who did this job, and her queue was always longer because she was more flexible in her approach than her colleague.

"Sure if the chorus girls want a wee extra beauty spot or darker eyebrows, I just give them what they want. What harm is it?"

But my memory showcases the two sisters in serious mood singing Moore's lovely words in stirring counterpoint, and I think it's a fitting commentary upon the pleasure and pain of a dander along memory lane.

> *On Lough Neagh's bank, as the fisherman strays,*
> *When the clear cool eve's declining,*
> *He sees the round towers of other days*
> *In the waves beneath him shining.*
> *Thus shall memory often, in dreams sublime,*
> *Catch a glimpse of the days that are over,*
> *Thus, sighing, look through the waves of time*
> *For the long-faded glories they cover.*

Freats, Treats and Fancies

Aideen, aged six or seven

"Mrs. Ritchie, have you finished with the pancake sieve? Me ma needs it."

"Och, God, daughter, I gave it to Veronica about ten minutes ago."

"Veronica, me ma needs the pancake sieve."

"Away up to Maggie Heyburn and see if she has it, I gave it to her just there now."

"Maggie, have you the sieve for me ma?"

"Didn't I lend it to Annie Donnelly – or maybe it was Lily. Go and see."

And by the time you got back, footsore and cross, the frothy pancakes would be sliding off the pan right onto your plate, magically made perfectly without the aid of the elusive sieve, but you were too far up to the elbows in butter to reflect upon that. It was the Shrove Tuesday ritual, when children were sent from house to house in vain pursuit of the pancake sieve, which had always moved on just before you arrived. The pattern was repeated year after year with new swathes of youngsters, or yout-lins, as my mother called them, and the older ones never let them into the secret. It was a rite of passage, a part of growing up. In later years my amazement focused on the fact that no matter how many kids came in search of the sieve, none of the adults ever lost their temper!

In Passage, too, they used to send young lads off on wild goose chases, for things like a tin of compression, a bubble for a spirit level, but they met their match in the cub who, on being asked to go for a barrowful of air, offered, "I'll push it if you fill it."

He was cut from the same cloth as the boy who used to do a paper round in Magherafelt. He was stopped one day by the schoolmaster who chided him for his brusque delivery methods.

"You shouldn't just roll the paper up and fling it at the house," he told him. "You should walk up the path, knock on the door, and hand it into the hand of the person who opens it to you." The lad considered a minute, and then suggested,

"All right, then. I'll let on to be you, and you can let on to be me, and you show me how it's done."

The master was delighted to oblige, and took pains to act civil-ly, coming up the path, tapping on an imaginary door and hand-ing over the paper with a smile.

The boy took the paper, put his hand into his pocket, and handed the messenger a sixpence.

Nostalgia lends a gloss to our memories, I know that, and maybe we didn't have more fun in times gone by. Maybe we just had more time for each other. Everyone worked hard, but we knew how to place a value on our leisure hours. Families spent time together, maybe going for a walk, or sitting down to eat at the same time. The fare might have been simple, but the family tie was strong. I used to walk along the old railway track with my dad, deep in conversation, and many a summer evening we ambled down the back towards Smith's fields to hear the corn-crake's weird and lonely cry. I didn't even know the phrase then, but that was quality time!

We once took a trip to Gortin in Uncle Charlie's station wagon, usually referred to as 'Tom' because of its registration letters, TOM 189. 'Tom' was actually an Austin A40 estate car, a prototype of which only two were made, built at the Cowley motor works near Coventry, and it held eight of us, because Auntie Ann had had the brainwave of taking the cushions off her three-piece suite and laying them down in the back of the vehicle, and here cousin Frank and I reposed like little Pharaohs, snug as a bug in a rug and twice as comfortable. Business class? We had the best seats in the house.

When we had exhausted the sights of this village in dark Tyrone, we went in search of a drop of tea, and sought the advice of two old dears, who immediately offered to provide the necessary themselves. We accepted gratefully, but only later realised that they didn't actually have a tea-shop. They had just spotted a chance to make a few bob from the tourists, and we were fed tea and Indian bread at vast expense in their own front parlour. They regarded our mode of transport and the almost empty street and informed Charlie,

"You can park you beach wagon there, sir, and it'll be quite safe."

I remember that day with deep affection and amusement. The taste of the Indian bread is with me still, yet all the gourmet meals we've enjoyed over the years have blended into a gastronomic kaleidoscope where nothing stands out.

Nowadays the mantra is work hard, play hard. I sometimes wonder if it should be work hard, take it easy. We have forgotten how to relax, and no longer take delight in simple things.

Daily activity when I was young had a pattern to it, that changed with the seasons, and focused on festivals and the great events of life – birth, marriage, and death. We always made New Year resolutions – and always broke them! At Easter we rolled our eggs down Murray's Hill, and if the grass was dry enough, rolled ourselves after them, and got up early on the Sunday to see the sun dancing at daybreak.

Hallowe'en was for freats and fortune-telling – roasting hazel nuts, reading the cards, eating an apple in front of the mirror, and washing your shift in a south-running stream. Many of the freats were connected with marriage and courtship, and many a bright eye and blushing countenance gathered round the fire to see what – or who – the future held in store.

The hazelnut ritual required every girl or boy to select a few nuts and line them up on the bars of the grate, assigning to each one the name of an admirer, or admiree! The subject of the experiment would then concentrate very hard on the nuts, while trying to ignore the teasing of the others. The first nut to blaze up was the person to whom your affection would be given in the following year.

If you love me, pop and fly!
If not lie there silently.

Another matchmaking ritual involved a pot full of water with a layer of clay or sand on the bottom. Into this the subject would press little scraps of paper bearing the names of boys or girls in the neighbourhood. By the flicker of firelight or candlelight, everyone would bend their concentration on the pot, and anon there would float to the surface one of the scraps. It would then be unwrapped with great excitement and much giggling, not to mention the disappointment if it did not contain the hoped-for name, and embarrassment if it did!

Not for the faint-hearted were the rituals of shift-washing and apple-eating. In the former, a girl was required to go out at midnight and wash her shift in a south-running stream. Going home, she would put it on a clothes horse before the fire to dry, and in the wee small hours, in would come the wraith or fetch of her future husband and turn it over for her! In the days before the idea of the new man was even a twinkle in Germaine Greer's eye, this probably represented the only time the man of the house would busy himself about the washing, but far be it from me to spoil a romance!

Another way to spy out your fate was to stand before a mirror at midnight and eat an apple by the light of a single candle. This time the shade of your husband-to-be would come up and stand behind you. Scoffers might say he was waiting for the butt, cynics that this was all a poor man could expect from the women – the leftovers.

If you failed to establish the identity of your future partner, this was probably because he hadn't yet entered your orbit. In this case, you went out into the garden, in a time when everyone grew a few vegetables, and, turning three times in a clockwise direction, closed your eyes and randomly selected a cabbage, which you then pulled up by its roots. If it came up easily, you would marry soon; if it was a fine specimen, why then you would get a handsome man; and even better, if it had a good bit of clay clinging to its roots, he wouldn't be short of a bob or two! My attention was always focused upon getting one without a fine fat slug clinging to it!

For more general fortune-telling, there was the ritual of the plates. Six plates or saucers were arranged upon a table, one bearing a button, one a wedding ring, one some water, one a handful of clay, one a sixpence, while one was left empty. Each person would stand blindfolded before the table while the plates were shifted about so that their exact order could not be memorised, then tentatively each questing hand would hover uncertainly over the array before finally settling on one plate. The ring meant marriage, the button, spinsterhood or bachelordom. Water meant you would travel far and wide, the sixpence, that you would be well-off, the empty saucer indicated that the future was uncertain. But the clay meant you would be dead within the year, and many's the time I saw my mother surreptitiously move the clay-filled plate out of the way lest an unwary hand should chance upon it, for although no one actually believed in these old customs, still, it was nice when they augured well.

We always emulated good old Aunt Jane and baked a ring in an apple tart, a culinary speciality of my mother's, who made the best apple tart I've ever tasted, and she always put in a button and a sixpence too, so that more than one person got a share in the largesse. We never ducked for apples in our house, but the basement kitchen was transversed by a beam into which was driven a nail, and from this an apple was suspended by a string. You had to try to take a bite out of this with your hands tied behind your back. Not easy, but enormous fun!

There were rituals we would never do, but which were talked of in hushed tones, the same way the obligatory ghost stories were told. These included anything to do with graveyards, and the curious custom of rolling the lead, which I have never seen and only vaguely understand. Apparently it is possible to run a small amount of molten lead into water, allowing it to form a shape, and this again will give you an indication of how your future might pan out. We were often regaled with the salutary tale of a girl who did just this and the shape formed was a coffin, indicating her early demise. The delicious frisson of fear this produced was more than compensated for by the roaring fire, the hunks of barm brack and the huge mugs of tea that kept out more than the autumnal chills.

Oddly, the bedtime ritual of the egg carried no scary connotations. If you managed to fit in all the other scrying exercises before or just on midnight, and had any energy left, you could check on how your future partner was shaping up in one of two ways, both, if you were of the belt and braces mentality.

First you got a glass of water and an egg. You pricked the pointed end of the egg with a pin and made a hole just large enough to let the white flow out, and this you directed into the water with as steady a hand as you could manage. When it was done, you placed the glass on a south-facing window sill, and in the morning the white would have formed itself into a shape that would allow you to figure out your future husband's profession or occupation – a quill might indicate an academic; a cart, a farmer; a hammer, a joiner or workman. Of course, if you already had someone in mind, you could always argue that you saw something completely different! And last thing before you went to sleep, you would take the salt cellar and shake salt all along the bed foot, intoning as you did so:

> *Salt, salt, I sow thee*
> *In the name of God and Eternity,*
> *If I get a man and a man gets me*
> *In my first dream may I him see,*
> *The colour of his hair and the coat he'll wear,*
> *And the day he'll be wed unto me!*

But you had to be sure that everything else was in order before you did this one, for if you spoke a word after doing it, the spell was broken!

My very favourite Hallowe'en tradition was *Doing Ruth*, because for me, this talk of suitors and future husbands was all very well, but there were a great many other things in the world that I wanted to know, and Ruth had an answer for them. To 'do Ruth', you needed a Bible, a piece of string, and a widow's key, and furthermore, the practice worked best if the widow's key had been stolen! There were several widows in and around the Donaghmore Road in my young days, including my grandmother, and oddly enough, they all seemed to make a habit of leaving their keys in the door coming up to October 31st! Of course, we're not talking about those tiny little apologies for keys that Mr. Yale invented, nor even the bigger but still slender things that go with a mortise lock. No, we're talking six inches of solid metal such as the gaoler in the Tower of London might rattle on his belt, the kind that today would cost twenty five pounds to copy and require two hands to turn, producing that satisfying thunk! that tells you the door is well and truly locked, without the need to push against it with your bum in case the latch didn't engage!

Having assembled the components, it was necessary to tie the key into the Bible at the first page of the Book of Ruth. I remember watching my mother performing this ritual, and being convinced that there was something arcane and mystical in the very swirl of the cord and the knots she tied. Two people then sat opposite each other, holding the book between them at arm's length by balancing the key on the tip of the middle finger of their right hands. One would ask Ruth a question, the answer to which must be a clear Yes or No. Ruth didn't deal in subtleties! Thus, you couldn't ask how many children will I have? But you could say will I have more than one... more than two... and so on. As my dad used to say, there's more ways of killing a cat than choking it with butter. Then, concentrating fiercely, both parties would recite,

And Ruth said, entreat me not to leave thee, nor to return from
following after thee, for whither thou goest, I will go, and whither
thou lodgest, I will lodge; thy people shall be my people,
and thy God, my God.

If the answer was No, the Bible hung there as steady as a rock, but if the answer was Yes, it would turn firmly clockwise. A counter-clockwise turn indicated uncertainty, but this result was rare. I have seen this ritual performed hundreds of times, have taken part in it over many years, and I can safely say that I have no idea why it should move on some occasions and stay steady on others, yet such is the case. Of course you can make it turn, and we sometimes did, when you asked something for the crack and everyone knew you were doing it; but on most occasions the participants were deadly serious, and the book turned willy-nilly, unaided by human agency, at least on a conscious level. Maybe it's to do with telekinesis or the power of the mind, but such concepts were alien to us in the first half of the last century. I was much intrigued to discover many years later that the ritual was once widely used in Scottish law courts when decisions proved hard to reach, and it was treated with the greatest reverence and belief.

———— ∞ ————

The best of all possible celebrations was Christmas, the only time of year when you could buy, never mind afford, turkey or goose – no deep freezers then! A few days before Christmas Eve we bought a plain loaf to make the stuffing. If it was allowed to go slightly stale before using, it would crumble easily without stickiness. Nowadays it would be blue-moulded long before you needed it. In my mother's young days, her aunt Brigid, who lived in Ballymulderg and owned a thriving farm, used to send a goose every year. It would come, plucked and oven-ready, the day before the holiday, in a large cardboard box, surrounded by an array of home-grown vegetables – leeks, onions, parsley, and of course, the spuds – all delivered by a smiling Ulsterbus driver who brought it right to the door with a cheery, "There's yer Christmas dinner for ye now!" as he dropped it off.

We went up the town every Christmas Eve, and my father always bought something new for the festive season – glasses, napkins, something small but pretty. I remember the year he presented me with a box of mandarin oranges. There were six of them, each individually wrapped in purple tissue paper, nestling in little moulded hollows of egg-box cardboard, also purple, inside a box with a flip-top lid. It was luridly embellished in shades of orange and mauve, giving it a very exotic flavour. I had to be persuaded to eat them eventually, for their look and aroma was enough for me, and I didn't want to spoil the symmetry by taking one out of its nest. Somehow, the ones I buy today in a synthetic net in Tesco never taste the same.

The back bedroom on the first floor in our house had an enormous mirror on one wall. It was left over from the days when my mother had her hairdressing salon, and I realise now that it was quite beautiful, being mounted in mahogany and almost filling the entire wall. Then it just seemed a handy thing for my mum to check if the seams of her stockings were straight! One Christmas Eve, when I was about three, my dad found a piece of chalk lying about, and just for fun, he wrote *Merry Christmas, Aideen!* across this mirror. He promptly forgot about it, but I, going into the room some time later, was absolutely and immediately convinced that the message had been written by Santa Claus, and that it presented incontrovertible proof that he would be there later with my presents. For years afterwards, Daddy had to find an opportunity on December 24th to write a message on the mirror, for until it appeared I was like a hen on a hot griddle, in an agony of uncertainty, but yet it could not appear too early or the magic would be dissipated. I used to creep in and out of that room all day like a stalker, and many were the subterfuges dreamed up to keep me occupied for long enough to allow the deed to be done, for I was constantly under the feet of the adults.

One year I received a pair of pale blue brushed nylon pyjamas from my great-aunt Lil, a veritable luxury, with an embroidered satin collar and cuffs. I was allowed to put these on early and prance about the house in them, probably as a bribe, or a scheme to divert my attention. The ruse worked. I was so intent on the impression created by my *dishabillé* that I quite forgot to worry about the message. I dandered into Mum's room to admire myself in her dressing-table mirror, which was more my size than the big one, and distinctly heard a tap on the window pane. Since the window was at least twelve feet off the ground, I knew this was not my dad playing tricks on me. I turned towards the big mirror – and there it was! *Merry Christmas, Aideen!* in flowing script, such as no human being could possibly produce. I ran out of the room in an ecstasy of joy and wonderment, that Santa Claus should take all that trouble to assure me of his coming, and then to alert me to what he had done, in case my vanity got in the way.

Comfort and joy? I had it in spades. I would give anything to have some of it back now, when so much has changed, so much has been lost. Where today would you find a fire-grate with bars broad enough to accommodate a row of hazelnuts? Where a child that watched for mystic messages on a mirror? Where, for that matter, would you find a south-running stream?

Where a corncrake?

Gaslight

Martin Fahy

It was a relic from the days of gas lighting, the street light outside our front door, one of those old-fashioned upright ones that you'd pay a fortune for now, if you could find one in Wilson's salvage yard. It was a favourite pastime of local kids to hold onto this with one hand while executing a circular dance of ever-increasing velocity, until your hand got so warm you had to let go, spiralling off into the wide blue yonder. But in those days, there was always someone to catch you. On Christmas Eve, the Salvation Army band went round the town playing carols, and by the time they made it as far as the Donaghmore Road, the night would be drawing in. They always stopped right outside our door, under the light, and when you heard the strains of *Silent Night* from trumpet and horn, you were in no doubt that God was in his heaven, and all was right with the world.

The town lights went out at a quarter to twelve every night, and it was considered very risqué to be caught out on the streets after that time. It acted as a kind of unofficial curfew. If you were visiting friends and stayed later than you meant to, some member of the family would offer to walk you home with a torch – one if male, at least two if female, for if there was one thing worse than being out after lights out, it was being out on your own! These were the days of shanks' pony, when only the doctor, the minister, and one or two very rich people like the schoolteacher had a car for everyday use. At Christmas time, the lights were kept on throughout the night for two nights, in deference to the season. When we consider the prevalence of stories about ghoulies and ghosties and long-nebbed beasties, we should reflect that where there is darkness there is also mystery, where there is shadow, there is the stuff of dreams. With the onslaught of the Troubles many things changed. Now when you didn't want to be abroad at night, the town lights remained on throughout the hours of darkness. It is an oddity of the human condition that we can and do get used to anything, and it wasn't until I moved back to my country roots that I remembered how many stars the night sky could hold, and how much poorer I had been in not seeing them for years. I also remembered that the Man in the Moon had a face, and that the Milky Way shimmered on still evenings.

In my childhood we cooked by gas, and the supply into the houses was paid for via 'the shillingy meter', an ancient wall-mounted piece of apparatus where the supply could be temporarily disconnected by turning off a tap. It had to be constantly fed to keep the home fires burning. It was quite small, and as gas became more expensive we often had to call the gas man, Sammy Weir or Billy Reilly, to come and empty it so that we could start feeding it (and ourselves!) again. We had a gas iron, too, a massive contraption that was connected to the supply by means of a rubber hose linked to the cooker, sporting a naked flame in its malodorous depths. I was terrified of this monster, and would take any detour available so as not to have to pass near it on ironing day. There was a combined smell of rubber and gas that spelt terror to me, and to this day, anything remotely resembling that smell has my stomach in reminiscent knots. My Uncle Wilf made me a wee wooden ironing board, a perfect miniature in every respect down to its folding legs and rest for the iron, but much as I loved it, I could never be persuaded to use it in even remote proximity to the genuine article.

The meter required a one shilling coin to activate it, and coming up to weekends and holidays you made sure there was a plentiful supply of single shillings to feed the ever-hungry maw. At Christmas time they were stock-piled for weeks. One night there came a knocking at our front door and my grandmother opened it to find Mandy, the daughter of the house next door, who was then about nine or ten, blond, bonny, and full of purpose. She presented a two-shilling piece with the request,

"Me Ma says would you be able to give her a single shilling for the meter?"

My grandmother produced her purse, wherein she found not one, but two, single shillings which she handed over with a smile. Two minutes later, the door knocked again. It was Mandy.

"Sorry to bother you, Mrs. Campbell," she apologised, "but which one is the single one?"

My Great-Uncle Tom, who lived in Irish Street, had a housekeeper, a lady from the country who talked through her teeth, kept her money in a knotted handkerchief at the bottom of a suitcase stored under her bed, for fear of 'townies', and who had never married. Having failed to capture the man of her dreams, she refused to settle for second-best, saying, "Rather a clane fast before a dirty supper."

Tom had gas lighting in his house, and one day he asked my grandmother whether it was normal to have to replace the mantles every day. They were not merely deteriorating, he told her, but completely disappearing. Granny assured him this was unusual to say the least, but it was not until many weeks later that the explanation presented itself. Passing through the hallway, she caught sight of the housekeeper perched on a chair attacking the light fitting with a frenzied energy. Seeing my grandmother staring at her, she offered, by way of explanation,

———— ∞ ————

"Them dirty big spiders! Me heart's broke getting rid of them cobwebs! You'd nivver see spiders like this in the country."

The lights going out around midnight presented all sorts of difficulties for those of a nocturnal disposition, who liked to make their ceilidh late. Our good friend Martin came to collect a birdcage for his young brother, Tony, who had acquired, willy-nilly, a budgie, when it flew into the kitchen one day and refused to leave. A cage was produced from somewhere, but it was on the small side, and it wasn't long before all the experts, ourselves included, gave it as our opinion that the poor bird could do with a bit more space to exercise, and a few more toys to help it pass the time. I had once been given a budgie for a present, and a more uninteresting pet I found it hard to imagine, unless it might be a goldfish. But at least a fish would allow you to amuse yourself by telling gullible friends that it was a rare piranha hybrid, vicious and carnivorous. Then you could watch them dangle a tentative finger over the bowl in a kind of horrified fascination to see if the critter was tempted to leap for live flesh. Many years after Joey had gone to the great maize-field in the sky, the cage remained, a reminder of my ingratitude: four feet high, a-jingle with mirrors, perches, bells and motley, and best of all, a life-size plastic bird that we had been advised to provide to keep the feathered one from feeling lonely. Later I wondered if it might have had quite the opposite effect, driving the bird insane with frustration by refusing to yield to blandishments, batterings, and outright abuse with even one single chirp, but what do I know?

Martin arrived at a respectable time to collect the cage, but after numerous cups of coffee, several packs of cigarettes, and much crack, the Rubicon was passed and the town lights were out, but home he had to go eventually, walking, of course. This was the early years of the Troubles, and after some debate it was deemed wiser not to wrap the cage up, in case he should encounter an army patrol, and be supposed to be carrying a suspicious package. In any case, if they opened it up, he would have to cope with the discarded wrapping, so naked it would remain. He

———— ∞ ————

left our house about three in the morning in a thick November fog, assuring us that he would be quite safe, for the jingle of the numerous bells would alert any oncoming traffic to his approach. As he went along Thomas Street, past the DHSS offices where there was a permanent checkpoint, he was hailed by the soldier on graveyard shift, who, peering out from the relative warmth of the sanger, saw a tall young man striding out athletically, swinging a bird cage, in which perched, to all intents and purposes, a fine specimen of blue and white budgiehood. He checked. He stood. He retreated a few steps. He furrowed his brow, decided against too close an encounter. As Martin drew level with him, he called out,

"Taking your budgie for a walk then, mate?"

Martin twirled the cage, set the bird dancing. "Sure am," he replied. "The fresh air's terrible good for it."

Somewhere in England there is a middle-aged military man who insists that in Northern Ireland there are people who walk pet birds in the wee small hours in a swirling November fog – and no one believes him.

The lights going out could produce optical illusions of another nature. My mother had a friend called Anna (of whom more later) who ran a hairdressing salon. Mum used to go down to help out, since Anna was often so lovesick that she was quite unable to handle clients, but if half the stories are true, and I suspect most of them are, there was little work and much talk, and only a few hairs were dressed on an average day. Anna tended to leave her clients waiting for long periods while she slipped out to meet one or other of her admirers, and it wasn't the first time that her clients left the shop just before ten o'clock at night. The worst case was when a lady from the country came in to get a perm, and it was well after midnight before she was ready to leave. It was only then that she informed them that her bicycle had been left in McNaney's yard for safety, and when they all walked her up to collect it, they found, as Alfred Noyes's Highwayman did when he clattered and clanged over the cobbles to the inn, that all was locked and barred. Half of Anne Street was wakened before they could persuade Paddy to come and open up for them.

Once my mother was away so long that my grandmother sent Aunt Mona to look for her. Of course Mona got involved in the crack and it wasn't long before Anna's sister arrived, and more tea was made. Eventually Mona made a move to go, but Emily embarked on a last tidy up to be ready for the morning. She went over to the window to draw back the drapes, whereupon the night air was rent by a bloodcurdling shriek and Emily staggered back into the room white-faced and trembling, sobbing that there was a man hidden behind the curtains, with murder or worse on his mind. The four girls huddled together, petrified, waiting for the intruder to leap out and seize one of them by the throat. Nothing happened. A few agonising seconds elapsed before my mother said,

"Are you sure there was someone there? Should we take another look?"

Emily's response was another spine-tingling shriek, followed immediately by a frenzied hammering at the door.

"They're coming, they're coming!" sobbed Emily, while Anna fainted daintily and dramatically into a chair, but my mother, being made of sterner and more practical stuff, had figured out that (a) if there was a man hidden behind the curtains, he would hardly have stayed there when his cover was blown in so dramatic a fashion; and (b) he wouldn't be banging on the outer door if he was already inside. She strode over to the window and swept back the curtains, only to find herself staring into the anxious but un-murderous face of a worried policeman, shading his eyes with his hand as he stared in at them from outside. At once the knocking began again, and Mona, who had also put two and two together and figured it out, stepped over the prone Anna to open the door. Two tall RUC men stepped inside.

"What in the name of God is going on?" demanded one.

"We heard the screams and thought someone was being murdered," explained the other.

The explanation of course was quite simple. The two men were having a quiet smoke outside the lighted window of the salon, when Emily drew back the curtains and mistakenly believed them to be inside the room. Blissfully unaware of this, their time out was shattered by her shrieks, leading them to bang on the door in case someone needed rescued. After equilibrium was restored and more reviving tea made and drunk, one of the officers said, "We'd better get you wee girls home."

Anna and Emily lived a stone's throw away but my mother and Mona had a fair wee bit to walk to the Donaghmore Road, so they were grateful for the offer, but when it turned out that they were being invited to drive home in a police car, they declined firmly.

"No harm to ye," said Mona, "but if we were seen getting out of a police car on the Donaghmore Road, we'd never live it down. People would think we'd been lifted."

No amount of persuasion would change their minds, so in the end they walked home, with the police car crawling slowly behind them all the way until they reached the safety of their own door and slipped inside.

Who said the idea of community policing was a new one?

Laughter and Tears

Betty O'Neill, one of 'The Circle'

Biddy was so fat that she frequently got stuck in the chair, for she insisted on sitting in one of those old-fashioned farmhouse style carvers, saying it was good for her back. She had an immensely volatile personality and could go from laughter to tears in seconds, often within the same sentence. She was never afraid to laugh at herself, as on the memorable occasion when we were playing spin the bottle in our kitchen, and Wilf gave her the forfeit of touching her toes. I don't know who laughed more, Biddy or her audience. Many years before when Wilf was only a cub he had been sent to Biddy's for a message, and found her chasing one of her offspring round the kitchen threatening death or disfigurement if she caught him. She was armed with a dangerous weapon – the cotton belt of her dress. The miscreant fled as Wilf came in, and Biddy collapsed in floods of tears, bemoaning the child's behaviour and the death in infancy of another son who, she asserted, would never have given her so much trouble.

"And I wouldn't care," she sobbed, "only I don't think he was baptised so he's probably in Limbo!"

Wilf, at a loss as to how he should respond to these concerns, offered what comfort he could.

"Och nivver mind, Biddy. Many's the time my mother wishes I was in Limbo."

The tears turned to gales of laughter quicker than you could blink.

Her natural exuberance stood her in good stead many a time, for her husband was a man who, like many men in the '50s, worked away from home, having 'taken the boat' to England, and supported the family via weekly postal orders. The only trouble with Johnny was that the interval between stipends might vary from one week to six, and Biddy was often in serious financial difficulties, but she remained cheerful and tearful in equal measure. Her generosity was as monumental as her figure. She called with us once and for some reason decided that I should have a treat. I have no idea why. Maybe I had recently had a birthday, made my first Communion, or merely got a good mark in my homework, but nothing would do but that I should accept a shiny two shilling piece, a fortune to me. My mother was torn between not wanting to deprive Biddy of her housekeeping money, and fear of insulting her by refusing the gift, but she insisted that it was far too much and a penny would do just fine. Biddy smiled and assured her that the postal order had come that day and all was well. It was only later, accidentally and without guile, that she let slip the total amount of the payment – four shillings and sixpence.

The neighbours all kept an eye out for her welfare, and one day my mother was sent in to see if she was all right, for she hadn't been seen out for several days. She found her ensconced beside a blazing fire, in great good humour. The postal order had been cashed and there was food on the table. My mother reflected that she must also have been able to buy coal, but then noticed that the flames were dying away very quickly. The mystery was solved when Biddy reached down and calmly tore a strip of lino off the floor and hurled it into the fireplace, where it blazed up ardently. Only then did mum notice that the chair whereon her hostess sat was resting on a tiny island of linoleum that was getting smaller by the minute, the rest of the floor having been stripped down to the bare concrete to feed the flames. Biddy's father was less than sympathetic to her plight, telling her that since she had had the bad taste to marry a man whose bottom lip hung over his waistcoat like a side of bacon, she deserved all she got. She herself had a lovely face framed by dark wavy hair, and warm brown eyes, despite her weight problem which was probably exacerbated by the diabetes that plagued her in later life.

Old Jack, her father, was a man of strong convictions and even stronger language. He swore copiously and fluently at the slightest provocation, and his combination of cuss words was legendary, only rivalled by a man of my father's acquaintance who was in the merchant navy. It was said of him by a shipmate that he sailed from the port of Liverpool with a cargo of lignum vitae bound for Tierra del Fuego, swore all the way out and all the way back, and never repeated himself once. Jack and the family were awakened one night by a mighty thunderstorm that had put out all the lights in the town. They huddled by candlelight in the kitchen while Jack sprinkled holy water and prayed loud and long, asking God to protect them all for they were the best family a man could have. Unfortunately he then fell over a chair, for the little candle was not throwing its beams far enough that night, whereupon he turned nasty and called them for all the ****** he could think of, calling down Hell and damnation on their heads, and insisting,

"Etarnal Jaysus, they're the worst pack of ****** a man could have for a family, what the Hell good are they to anybody?"

The Dean of the parish, who I think at the time was Dean McDonald, took great crack out of Jack, saying he never committed a sin with his swearing for it was totally unconscious and merely habitual. He enquired, none too seriously, if Jack had ever thought of joining the Down and Connors, one of the Temperance Societies that thrived in the early decades of the twentieth century. Jack withered him.

"Etarnal Jaysus, Dean, I'm only fit for the down and outs."

Jack worked as commissionaire at the local cinema, and my mother remembered that despite his irascible manner he had a soft spot for 'nice youngsters' and many a time allowed her and her pals to slip in at the back of the picture house when they didn't have enough money to pay at the door. Later, as teenagers, they preferred to do things in style and sit in the stalls whenever they could. The balcony was only for the wealthy, being sixpence a time, or for when you were older and being escorted by a beau. Uncle Wilf had the right idea: he went to the pit, and so could afford three nights' viewing for their one. Unfortunately, if he happened to be there the same night as they were, he spoiled their enjoyment by standing up during the interval when the lights came up and hailing them loudly from below, while they tried to pretend they didn't know him. On other nights he and a few pals would wait till the show started, then borrow the bikes that were lined up outside belonging to the older fellows who were enjoying the offering on the big screen. They would spend a happy hour or two cycling round the town, making sure to leave everything back before the pictures came out.

One night when Jack was clearing up after the show he found a pair of gloves in the toilets, rolled one inside the other as you do with socks. There being no obvious owner around to return them to, he put them in his pocket meaning to leave them in the box office, but forgot all about them and went off home. After he had eaten supper he and his wife were sitting comfortably on either side of the fire, like two eggs waiting to boil, when he noticed a foul smell. He sniffed the air, and looked about him. There was nothing to explain it, but it grew worse as he sat. Unbeknown to him, his wife had smelt it too, and she was also trying to locate the source. After a while Jack could stand it no longer.

"What in the name of ****** is that ****** smell?"

His wife was as gentle as he was aggressive. "I don't know Jack. I thought it was you."

"Suffering Jaysus, it's not me, Hell roast ye. Are you sure it's not you?"

"Och naw, Jack, it's not me."

There followed a few minutes of tense searching about, then Jack put his hand in his pocket and pulled out the gloves. When he unrolled them and realised what they had been used for, he understood why they had been left behind in the toilets and not put back on the owner's hands where they belonged. He hurled them into the fire with an accompanying oath and a long description of said owner's pedigree.

"Etarnal Jaysus, the dirty ******!"

"Och never mind Jack, sure it's all right now," soothed his wife. Jack glared at her.

"It's all right surely," he agreed, "but there was I sitting thinking you had committed yourself."

Jack had another daughter, Milly, who was walking out with a young man who was in the army. When he was away on active service, Milly prayed constantly for him, much to Biddy's disgust and annoyance, for the sisters shared a room and the nightly ritual disturbed Biddy's sleep. The final straw was when Milly took over a corner of the landing to construct a May altar to Our Lady, and spent hours on her knees praying for Ted's safe return. Biddy felt that this was going a bit far, so one day before the hour of prayer, she stole up the stairs and hid in the bedroom. During a pause in her devotions, when Milly was begging the Blessed Virgin to send her love home to her waiting arms, Biddy murmured in sweet gentle tones, *"Yes, Milly!"*

Instantly Milly was on her feet, charging down the stairs two at a time screaming that the Blessed Virgin had spoken to her. Biddy was convulsed with mirth, but it soon became clear that Milly was hysterical and nothing would calm her, so a neighbour was dispatched to get her father out of work. Jack arrived within minutes, breathless with imprecations, and almost as upset as his offspring.

"Etarnal Jaysus, me daughter has religious mania! Suffering Jaysus, send for the priest. To hell with him, send for the bishop!"

This was too much for Biddy, who could no longer contain her laughter, but on hearing the noise, Jack immediately decided that to add insult to injury, they now had a burglar in the house. Grabbing the brush he was off up the stairs, and diving into the room where Biddy was ineffectually trying to hide behind the door he grabbed at her, roaring in triumph, "I've got the bastard!"

The drubbing he had in store for the burglar was as nothing to what Biddy got when all was revealed.

In my mother's courting days she had an acquaintance called Boyd Greason, an American, well-known to the seven girls[2] who palled around together and called themselves 'The Circle'. None of them fancied Boyd in the slightest, though he seemed to regard himself as the answer to a maiden's prayer, but his determination to get himself a girlfriend gave them many an excuse for a bit of crack. They were constantly fending off his advances, but he hovered on the edge of things, willing to do anything that might ingratiate him into the inner circle. One night my mother and Shona Campbell decided to dress him up and send him up to Biddy's, so with his full co-operation they gathered together an outfit that would fit him, high shoes, a trench coat, and one of my mother's turbans. My mum, who as part of her training as a hairdresser had studied beauty culture, did his make-up, and soon, complete with dramatic eyes, scarlet lips, and a beauty spot, he set off. Mona was already planted in Biddy's to report on the effect, and by all accounts it was much more startling that anyone could have anticipated.

[2] Maureen, Mona, Shona and Una Campbell, Betty O'Neill, Lila Carberry and Veronica Rice

———— ∽ ————

Boyd had been told to ask whether a Mr. J. M***** lived here, and Biddy, completely fooled by the disguise and clocking Boyd's trans-atlantic accent, immediately took it into her head that here was someone with whom her hapless husband was having an affair across the water, though to my knowledge he never did anything of the kind, and she began by berating the stranger and calling 'her' for all the harlots and loose women she could think of. When she had exhausted her store of abuse she turned back into the house for the poker, and pursued Boyd up the street, only her weight preventing her from overtaking him, handicapped as he was by three-inch heels, a skirt, and a fear of meeting anyone who knew him.

My grandmother once unearthed an old pullover of Charlie's, one of those V-necked sleeveless things, that had washed big, and bade my mother offer it to Biddy, whom she had met going up the street one bitterly cold day without a hap. In those days you wasted nothing, for if you couldn't use it, someone else could. It was drilled into me that 'wilful waste makes woeful want', and that if I wasted food, especially, I'd be forced to 'follow the hungry crows' in the future. Anyway, after a few more chilly days had passed there was no sign of Biddy wearing the pullover, and Granny began to worry that she might have inadvertently caused offence. Once more, my mother was dispatched to gather intelligence.

"My mother was wondering," she began, going for the jugular, "whether the pullover fitted you?"

Biddy beamed. "It did surely, Maureen daughter, and a quare warm one it is too."

"You weren't offended," she pursued, "you know, that she gave it to you?"

"A daycent woman like you mother? Indeed I wasn't, Maureen. I nivver have it aff me. It fairly keeps me back warm."

My mother must have shown her scepticism, possibly frowned a little, for all of a sudden Biddy began to shake with mirth and was soon doubled up with the force of it. Finally she sobered and wiped her eyes.

"Sure you don't believe me, but honest to God it's true. Look!"

And she hoisted her skirts to reveal a large maroon pullover doing duty as a pair of bloomers, explaining to my mother's horrified face that she didn't even need to make alterations, for the armholes were in exactly the right place.

Needless to say, my grandmother never believed it.

Biddy shared a house for a while with her sister-in-law, Cissie, whom my mother nicknamed Olive Oyl, and if you've never seen a Popeye cartoon, then I'm afraid I can't help you!

Cissie was long and thin, with lank dark hair secured on either side of her pale face with two large hair grips, and she was fixated on skin and skincare, especially my Aunt Mona's, for she was lucky enough to have a Miss Pears complexion all her life. But on meeting anyone with even passably good skin, Cissie would drool and say in ecstatic tones,

"Whatten skin! What kind of soap do you use?"

She would then rush out and purchase a bar of the preferred brand, adding to a growing collection, and use it until the next acquaintance confessed a preference for some other kind.

She loved to be clean, and usually took a bath late at night in the cellar when everyone had gone to bed. Very few people in those days had got around to converting the cellars, so in Cissie's case part of it was also used for its original purpose of storing coal. One morning, when she broke with tradition and had her bath first thing, she was surprised by a heavy tread coming down the stairs and remembered with horror that it was coal day, and here was Mick coming with the weekly delivery. He was as appalled as she was, confronted with the spectacle of a bath-bound Cissie, frozen into immobility, no doubt with a bar of some recently-purchased soap clutched in her skinny hand. Mick, known for his dourness, said the first thing that came into his head.

"Where do you want this coal?"

Released from her stupor by the sound of his voice, Cissie leapt out of the bath and made for the stairs, but Mick was before her, and, despite being a large man, showing surprising fleetness of foot. It was later said by those who knew that both of them burst out upon the rest of the family assembled in the upstairs kitchen with nothing to separate them but a few soapsuds.

It always amazed me that so many people on the Donaghmore Road kept lodgers, and I remain convinced that they could, by some arcane method known only to a few, subtly alter the physics of the houses to enable them to hold more than was humanly possible. Of course this was in the days when no one minded sharing; when en-suites were something you might find in a box of chocolates; and as long as you had a roof over your head and a bite to eat, you were content. The night before my mother was married the house was bursting at the seams, for Charlie and Anne had arrived with a young Maureen and Margaret, and my Dad's cousin Tom Sheerin who was to act as best man was also there. The door knocked.

"My name's Larry, and I'm a friend of Wilfred Campbell's. He told me if ever I was passing through and needed a bed, just to call with his family…"

Well, sure you couldn't put a man out on the street, now could you?

A friend of mum's had a lodger for whom she provided an evening meal at a cost of two pounds per week. He was terribly hard to please and the poor woman never knew what reception her offering might receive, and consequently was on tenterhooks every day until the repast was over. One evening, being a bit short of money, she prepared two boiled eggs and some fresh bread, enough to satisfy many a diner, but she had her doubts about him, so as soon as she set the food down in front of him she fled to the living room and shut the door. After a minute she heard the screech of a chair being pushed back from the table followed by the sound of hammering, and then the unmistakeable slam of the back door. When she plucked up enough courage to investigate, she found the untouched food banished to the far side of the table, and two pound notes nailed to the kitchen door.

Cissie had lodgers, a couple whose name I forget so I'll call them Smith, and a solo gent whose name I recall but who I'll call Jones. Mrs. Smith was seriously deranged, and was often to be seen running up and down the road in floating night attire *à la* Mrs. Rochester, but people got used to her. They used to hear her at night calling to her husband:

"Is everyone in?"

"Yes, dear."

"Is Cissie in?"

"Yes."

"Is Mr. Jones in?"

"Yes."

"Is Biddy in?"

"Yes."

"Are you in?"

"Yes."

"Then close all doors and close all windows."

One night, just as this refrain ended, there came a noise from below, quite possibly Cissie *en bain,* and there followed an agonised shout from the poor woman.

"Strike a light! Strike a light! There's someone still out! It's that poor orphan Cissie! Open all doors and open all windows!"

Another morning she approached my grandmother, enquiring if she had noticed anything wrong with the water supply. Nothing, granny assured her. Did she have a problem? Would she get Wilf to have a look at it?

"I don't think he could help, dear," said Mrs. Smith. "It's just that lately it's been coming with its hat and coat on it, and I don't think it's right."

One morning she waved down a bus travelling up the road,

then leapt in front of it. The driver made good work to get stopped without injuring her.

"What the hell do you think you're doing?" he glared at her.

She smiled. "Isn't it a beautiful morning, glory be to God!" she trilled.

"And you're a bloody eejit," he returned, as he moved off.

Mr. Jones proved to be a horse of a different colour, for in him, Cissie found her soulmate. He was long and lean with legs and feet like the letter L, and rejoiced in the nickname 'Bo', or possibly 'Beau'. I'm not at all sure that this was not bestowed by my mother as well. He was avant garde in the fashion stakes for he wore a scarf of such prodigious length that it could have included the whole household in its toils, and he used to let the ends hang down almost to his toes. Not until Tom Baker's Dr. Who many years later was a scarf of such wondrous dimensions seen in public. He was not very flash when it came to spending money, prompting my mother's comment that 'he would wrassle a monkey in a coalhole for a ha'penny', but this did not deter him from making a match with Cissie. The first anyone knew of it was when Biddy invited all the neighbours in for 'a big night', a term that covered a multitude but usually implied sandwiches, a cake or a few buns, and maybe a bottle of Guinness for the menfolk. The women of my childhood universally limited their drinking to a small sherry at wakes and weddings, so they made do with tea. Even such a simple arrangement was fraught with danger, however, as Granny Campbell found to her cost on one occasion when she was preparing for guests. She had my mother and Mona making sandwiches like they were going out of fashion, for above all, you didn't want to run out. When supper was served, as a drop in your hand for none of us had the luxury of a dining room, Maureen came in with a serving plate laden with sandwiches which she offered first to Gracie. She took in the plate at a glance, made a glam for it and set it on her knee with the immortal words, "Oh God, I couldn't ate all them!" and then proceeded to do just that. The other guests were so flummoxed they quite forgot to be hungry.

When the food had been disposed of in Biddy's, the sing-song started, and one minstrel there gave forth with a heartfelt rendition of *Moonlight in Mayo*. My Aunt Mona was seated between Cissie and Bo, and suddenly she felt the unmistakable touch of a hand upon her shoulder. She stiffened, but the hand progressed across her back, along the other shoulder, and down her arm. She considered her position. This was a woman not averse to standing up for herself, the woman who, as a girl in the Astor cinema in Georges Street, felt a hand upon her knee and realised the elderly man beside her was more interested in her than in the film. Too young to be afraid and merely annoyed at the interruption, Mona calmly undid the large pin in her kilted skirt, straightened it out, and brought it down full force upon the back of his hand. It cooled his ardour most effectively, but she didn't want to make a scene here and spoil Biddy's evening. Besides, she wasn't wearing her kilt. She moved forward slightly in her chair, and then enlightenment dawned, as Bo leant over behind her the better to caress Cissie's neck. Making her excuses, Mona removed to another chair, leaving the lovebirds to make eyes at each other uninterrupted.

After they were married they went to live in Birmingham. Once, when my mother was staying with her brother Charlie and his family, she went to visit them, and they decided to come back with her on the bus to see Charlie and the kids. On the journey, mum, seated in front of the happy pair, became uncomfortably aware of the conversation going on behind her, in which Cissie was insisting to Bo that there were two wee girls in this house, and he must give them something, it was only decent. Finding him an unwilling partner in the scheme, Cissie handed over two sixpences, with instructions that Maureen and Margaret were to have one each. When they arrived in Walford Road, Bo and Cissie were introduced to the family, and the two wee girls were given their gift – a threepenny bit each.

First Love

John Hazley

His name was John Hazley, and he lived at the top of our road. I was almost six, he a little younger, and he was a frequent visitor to our house, as was his grandfather, Christie.

I remember John very fondly, for two reasons. He and I were in my house one evening when my Uncle Wilf came in, and Wilf, who adored children, immediately got into the swing of our game, whatever it was. He was never one to shy away from the childhood world of make-believe, and it is one of the ironies of life that he, who would have made a great father, had no children of his own; but he enriched and enlivened many a childhood in a memorable and magical way. I remember one prized possession of mine was a small stove, which you could actually light, by means of a thick cotton wool pad soaked in methylated spirits, in the manner, I suppose, of an old-fashioned cigarette lighter. It had its own little pans in which you could boil water, and this I was doing one day, under careful supervision, fondly deluding myself, as only children can, that I was making soup. The only problem was that no one was willing to partake of it, the smell of the meths and the tinny taste from the pans effectively banishing all thought of hunger. Until Wilf. "I will surely, daughter," was his response when invited to try it. I offered it with all the confidence of Jamie Oliver in the local Comprehensive. He sipped. He slurped. He smacked his lips.

"I nivver tasted the like of that before," he replied, probably with complete accuracy. "Givvus another drop." If I remember correctly, he downed about five panfuls before the flame went out. Or someone blew it out.

On this occasion of John's visit, Wilf finally asked us to sing. I have never had any musical pretensions, and then, as now, would have swung from the light fittings rather than attempt a song, but John knew no such diffidence, lustily belting out *The Ballad of Tom Dooley* with rather more enthusiasm than skill. The rendition took the form of a semi-spoken verse and chorus, with only the name of the eponymous hero being shouted out at a volume that negated the need for amplification, and the effect was remarkable.

> *Hang down your head*
> *TAM DOOLEY!*
> *Hang down your head and cry;*
> *Hang down your head*
> *TAM DOOLEY!*
> *Poor boy you're bound to die.*

At the end, Wilf presented the minstrel with a shiny sixpence. John examined it for a moment, then looked at Wilf speculatively.

"Is she getting nothing?" he enquired, with a nod in my direction.

"No," Wilf told him. "Sure she wouldn't sing."

Now Wilf was generosity itself where I was concerned, and even at such a young age I knew the score. He was only keeping the crack going, and I would get my share later. But John would have none of it. There followed some tough negotiation, but Wilf held firm: no song, no money. Finally John gave up the argument, and abruptly took himself off without a word, leaving us agog as to where he might have got to. He returned a few minutes later from Tommy O'Neill's shop, where he had traded his sixpence for two threepenny bits, one of which he now handed to me, with a look at Wilf that would have reduced a lesser man to a simmering heap of ash.

My second memory of John is of his presenting me with my first bouquet – a large bunch of dandelions, carefully culled from 'round the back', and arranged by me in a jam-jar on the outside sill of the kitchen window, for I wasn't prepared to take the risk of bringing them into the house, even though their laxative powers were said to affect only those who actually picked them. But I was a cautious soul.

John, sadly, never found out if the old superstition was true, for the next day his young life was tragically cut short by a lorry delivering sand to the houses that were being renovated in Charlemont Street. Lorries were a source of great fascination to the wee boys, and they used to hang onto the back of the dumper trucks as they came down the hill, and try to jump off before the driver spotted them. On this occasion, John mistimed the jump, and did not reckon on the driver having to reverse into position. He died instantly, as the lorry backed over him, crushing his skull like an eggshell. The driver was as distraught as any one of us who knew and loved him. I remember the awful stillness that settled on the road, following the initial uproar when the tragedy was discovered. I recall the neighbours clustering round their doors, rooted to the spot, covering their mouths with their hands to stifle the horrified screams that were bringing the bile to the throat; his mother, running down the street as the news broke, her lovely sandy hair in disarray; and the many people who went out to stop her. I can still see the coat she was wearing, as clearly as if it were yesterday – a fitted brown woollen coat with darker brown frogging on the revere and a sprung skirt; and I can feel the shock, the shared sadness, the sense that not only Sheila, but the whole neighbourhood, had been bereaved, as indeed it had.

I was too young to refine upon the mystery of life and its brevity, but I remember watching the bunch of dandelions fade and wither, wondering how anyone so vital and lively could be gathering flowers one day, singing and laughing, and then simply not exist any more. It's a question I've never really found an answer to.

I hated it when we had to throw those dandelions away.

Christie always got his hair cut in Wee Joe's, a barber in Irish Street, much favoured by men who cared less about the cut of their jib than the necessity of chewing the fat and sorting out the problems of the world. In later years, my father numbered one of them. Many were the weighty matters upon which these rude philosophers held forth, and when the argument grew fierce and fearsome, one voice rose above the others and was deferred to, for Harte was a man widely acknowledged to be an authority on almost everything. But there was one dissenter in the ranks, and this was Christie, for he had long ago formed the opinion that if you wanted the definitive word on any subject under the sun, you had only to ask the Campbell girls on the Donaghmore Road, Maureen and Mona – my mother and my aunt.

He would arrive at our house about eleven in the morning, after a sojourn in Wee Joe's, and no matter what the girls were doing, they had to leave it and sit down, for Christie would not speak until he had their undivided attention. Once this was secured, he would begin.

"Are you sitting down, girl?"

"Right, Christie, we are; we're listening now."

"Would you believe him, girl?"

"Who, Christie?"

———— ∞ ————

"Och, ye know who I mean. Could he be right?"

"What about?"

"Och, dammit, ye must know. Harte says…"

And gradually it would emerge, the discourse, the claim, the counter-claim. The girls understood that it was their part to devise an argument to shoot down anything Harte might have to say, and this they could always do, for they loved to argue and debate among themselves, and they relished a challenge. They would worry away at the problem, then provide Christie with a quotation or a Biblical reference to support it, for Harte was not so good on the literary front, and these Christie would rehearse until he had them off pat, or at least the gist of them. Then he would sit back with a smile on his large, bland, good-looking face, and strike one portly fist into the palm of his other hand, grinning.

"By God, I'll hit Harte with that the morra!"

Only then could the girls break ranks and make lunch, but Christie wasn't hard to feed, liking nothing better than a cooking apple, peeled, and a mug of tea.

Christie had been one of my Uncle Charlie's circle before the latter went off to Birmingham, and they used to go for long walks out to Donaghmore or down the Carland Road past the old graveyard. One night they were accompanied by two other stalwarts, John and Seamus, and the dusk was just beginning to drop down as they approached the wall of the cemetery. All of a sudden, John took off at a hare's gallop, and after a glance at one other for enlightenment, which was not forthcoming, the rest followed at their usual pace. They caught up with him after about a mile, finding him panting and out of breath, and Charlie said,

"What in God's name is wrong with you, John? What happened you?"

John looked sheepish but was not about to admit to any loss of nerve relative to their surroundings.

"Can a man not run if he wants to?" he demanded.

———

If he had been in company with Wilf he might have fared less well. He was leaving a friend of ours home one night after her ceilidh and they too had to pass the graveyard. As they did so, Wilf offered Mary a cigarette, then patted his pockets distractedly. "I've no matches," he apologised, "but never mind, I'll get a light from this boyo standing at the wall." Needless to say there was no one standing at the wall, but Mary was home before Wilf had time to produce the matches he knew were in his pocket the whole time.

Around this time Christie had his eye on a fine lassie in town, but he thought she was somewhat out of his league.

"But I've figured it out," he told the boys. "I'm going to dress up as a rich American and get her interest, then we'll see how it goes."

Charlie wanted details.

"Here's the plan," Christie told him. "You and John are to be standing in Irish Street the morra and I'll go past in my disguise, and you see if you can spot me."

The boys took up their positions and waited, curious and attentive. Anon there came a familiar figure sauntering along the street, his broad shiny face shaded by a straw Stetson, but otherwise clad in his usual duds. He came right up to Charlie, grinned into his face, and swept off the hat with a fine flourish. "Wud ye know me, boy?"

As the man says, he would have known his guts on a thorn in America.

He complained to mum and Mona one night in June that he had a very bad back. "I blame it on the Mission," he told them.

"Why, Christie?"

"Och dammit, girl, sure you know why. Do you think I could stop now?"

"Stop what, Christie?" Sometimes they could work it out, but not always. This was one of those times.

"It was because I forgot the glasses."

"Right."

—— ∞ ——

"It was dark too. And I left out a blinjer. A blinjer! So I had to go back."

Two bemused Campbells exchanged glances. "Back where?"

He had set out to go to Confession during the Mission, in the previous October, and had made out a list of things he wished to discuss with the priest, but having forgotten his glasses, and the Confessional being but dimly lit, he had unwittingly left something out.

"But Christie," my mother explained, "You didn't need to go back, you left it out by mistake."

He shook his head. "But it was a blinjer, girl."

She let it go, remarking later that she doubted whether Christie had ever committed a 'blinjer' in his life, but no matter.

"So how did you get the bad back?"

"Well, when I hit him with the blinjer, he told me to say the Rosary every night for six months, and I couldn't let wee Sarah see me doing it, for then she would have figured out about the blinjer, and I wouldn't please her, so I sit up in bed at night and say it, and I think I've got a draught. Should I stop now?"

My mum and Mona looked at the kindly, anxious face, the earnest expression, and their desire to laugh at his innocence was quickly replaced by an appreciation of the innate goodness of men of his ilk, and the deeply-rooted faith that has kept many a soul from the clutches of evil by its rock-solid foundation.

"I'd say you could stop, Christie," Mona advised. "In the first place, I don't think any priest would have given you a penance like that, you must have misheard him."

"But it was –"

"– a blinjer. I know, but even so, I'd say he said six times at the very most, but even if he did say six months, you've done more than enough to make up for a rake of blinjers, so I'd stop right away."

His big face cleared. It was like the sun coming out from behind a cloud. "Right girl, I'll go by you! And I'll maybe buy a bit of red flannel to be on the safe side."

———

———— ∞ ————

At this stage of his life, Christie was living with his aunt, wee Sarah Gallogly, a tiny woman with enormous faith and a prayer for every occasion. Sometimes they fell out, mainly because Christie teased her and she didn't understand his humour; then she took it thick. On these occasions, she refused to call him by his name, and spoke only of 'my sister's son.' She told us how one night she lost her footing on the steep old stairs and fell in an untidy heap at the bottom of them. "My sister's son was standin' with his back to the range looking at me when I fell, and do you know what he said to me?"

"What, Sarah?"

"Come over here and I'll lift you."

She prayed non-stop, declaring "When God fails me, I'll go to the doctor," and once advised Wilf on the best way to pursue a favour in prayer. "You must ask the good St. Anne, to ask her blessed daughter, to invoke her glorious Son, to plead with His eternal Father, to grant your request."

He favoured her with a kindly but sceptical gaze.

"Sarah," he told her, "by the time I had got through that string of relatives, I would have forgotten what I wanted."

After the fall down the stairs, her own faith was tested to the limit. She had banged her face as she fell and, exacerbated by her advanced age, the bruising was severe. She showed the damage to my grandmother.

"I think you should show that to the doctor, Sarah," advised Granny, but true to her mantra, Sarah resorted to prayer.

"For," she explained, "them Campbell girls[3] are terrible good, and they gave me a statue of that wee black fellow, St. Martin. I'm doing a novena to him, and I'll not look at meself till it's finished."

About a week later, Granny opened the door to find Sarah, wrapped in a shawl, only the tip of her nose barely visible in the gloom. "Come on in, Sarah. How's the face?"

[3] The Charlemont Campbells, Una, Susie and Shona – lifelong friends, but no relation to Maureen and Mona

————

Sarah swept back the shawl in a gesture worthy of Garbo at her dramatic best. "How do you think it is?" she demanded. My grandmother was rendered speechless, for Sarah's wee face was black from ear to ear, but eventually she managed, "Do you not think you should see the doctor now, Sarah?"

"No!" she insisted. "I told you I was doing a novena to the wee black fella?"

Granny nodded, bemused.

"Well, I said I wouldn't look at meself for nine days, and the nine days were up this morning. I got a bit of a shock when I seen the result, but now I understand. He's curing me all right, but he's turning me into a black person like himself!"

Granny had a Sacred Heart altar and she used to burn a small oil lamp in front of it as a mark of respect. Sometimes the oil would run out and it might be a day or so before anyone got round to replenishing it, and it was always on days like this that Sarah arrived in. She would look askance at the lifeless lamp as she was about to take her leave and murmur a rambling rhyme that ended "... for us He died the Nazarene the crucified Missus your wee lamp's out!" just as she exited. It always sent them running for the oil bottle.

Strong as Sarah's faith was, it was a close run thing between her and a cousin of my grandmother's. Jinny's response to any form of adversity was to say three Hail Marys and there's no avoiding the fact that she got her prayers answered. One night she and my great-aunt Brigid were coming home from their ceilidh on bicycles when they were stopped by the police. Jinny had no light on her bicycle, in those days a fineable offence, and one that was considered serious enough by God-fearing and law-abiding citizens like her. She leapt off the bicycle, fell to her knees in the mud and cried out, "Brigid, Brigid! Say three Hail Marys they won't summons us!"

They didn't.

But she expected even more from the Almighty when she came into the kitchen in Ballymulderg one day just as Granny was trying to get Charlie to take his medicine, a putrid brew that left the child feeling sicker than before he swallowed it. Jinny took the bottle from Granny's hands and approached the boy.

"Say three Hail Marys it won't be bitter."

At one time in her life even the three Hail Marys weren't enough to save Jinny from a bit of controversy. Her family was involved in a dispute over a will, and a gathering of the clan was called for. She arrived in a pony and trap driven by her husband, but he wasn't allowed to be party to the discussions, it being for blood relatives only, so he was left standing outside, minding the equipage and his own business. When Jinny put in her claim for a share in the largesse one irate cousin shouted at her that she hadn't a hope.

"Didn't you get all you deserved when you got yon thing at the horse's head?"

Jinny was incensed. "What did I ever get at the horse's head?" she demanded.

"You know rightly what I mean. You got all you're going to get when you got the thing at the horse's head."

It was long before she realised that he meant her hapless husband, waiting patiently outside, minding the animal that would bring them both home.

As far as I know they enjoyed a happy marriage, even if she did have a tendency, when no baby-sitter could be found, to lock the children in the hen-house, but his brother Francie was less fortunate and once after a big row, his wife threatened to leave him. He came down to mull things over with Brigid, who, being a straight-talking woman, demanded to know if the wife had grounds for complaint or not. "What did you do, to make her so angry that she'd leave you?"

"She says I hit her, Brigid."

"Well, I hope you didn't, Francie. Is there any truth in it at all?"

He shifted uncomfortably. "I might have given her a bit of a shake comin' down the back loanin."

Brock

Mona and Aideen

"If you're finished with it, send it to the nuns. They'll know somebody who'll be glad of it."

Thus did my mother first instruct me on the virtues of recycling. "A narrow gathering gets a wide scattering," she advised, and though she hoarded things like letters and newspaper clippings, when it came to possessions, it was use it or lose it. We may live in a throwaway society but our parents did not. It went against the grain to throw anything other than undisputed rubbish in the bin, and nothing ever wound up there without regret. I didn't have anyone to hand clothes on to once I had outgrown them, so every now and then we would make up a bag of stuff and trundle it down to the Convent. This went for books that I had read, toys I had finished with, in fact, anything that wasn't pinned down, and it was customary when you got something new, to go at once and find something to hand on, since it wouldn't do to be spoiled. This ethic was so ingrained into my childhood psyche that to this day, whenever I buy something new to wear, I scour my cupboards to find something that can go to the charity shop. Old habits die hard? Don't you believe it. They hang on like grim death and never let go.

Anything that couldn't be handed on was recycled, re-modelled, or cannibalised. Nothing was wasted. An item of clothing that was past its best might be altered. A dress could be made into a skirt, a long-sleeved blouse into a short-sleeved one. My mother even re-modelled shoes, either by dying them to match an outfit other than the one they were originally bought for, or by cutting off straps or re-arranging them so that what started life as a shoe might end it as a sandal. She used nail polish as an embellishment to highlight interesting features, such as the peep-toe she created by removing scuffed toe-caps. This was perhaps less a virtue than a vice, prompted more by a desire for change than by the impetus to recycle, but who would have thought we had a latent Manolo Blahnik in our midst? As she might have said herself, it was a case of 'full many a flower is born to blush unseen.'

The '60s put paid to some of that activity, mind you, for after you had worn out a mini skirt, there was nothing left to recycle. In some cases there hadn't been enough for the skirt in the first place. My father used to comment on some of my compeers, "She wasn't wearing a mini, more of a Good Morning Judge." But in the '40s and '50s there was more to come and go on. When I was very small, about two or three years old, my Aunt Mona, whom I idolised, had a dress in grey cotton sprigged with dashes of red and white like a Jackson Pollock painting, with short sleeves offset by crisp white cuffs, and a stiff white collar. It had a full circular skirt, and when she sat on a low chair, I could crawl underneath its folds and hide, nestled against her knees. Many a time I fell asleep there and woke up in bed. She also had a skirt in vivid emerald green with two patch pockets which offered the same opportunity for refuge, but it never had the appeal of the grey dress.

Later on, when I had reached the stage of 'dressing up', she hoked out a gold lamé cocktail dress which had the luxury of a net underskirt, and with a couple of strategically placed darts and tucks, my mother made this wonder fit me, only – and this was an added bonus when you're playing Cinderella – it was floor length on me! My friends were pea-green with envy. At least I liked to think so. Later still, when 'stiff petticoats' were in, I had two of my own. One of these was made from blue foam, and it fluffed up your skirts nicely, but it didn't have the same cachet as the 'paper nylon' one which had to be ironed carefully to stiffen it, for it made a very satisfying rustle when you walked. I probably looked like one of those dolls whose fate it was to stand guard forever over a toilet roll, but at the time I was happy. Still, my heart always belonged to the gold lamé.

The wool cycle was also extended by the resourceful: hand knits were ripped out, the wool washed, and the worn bits saved to stuff cushions. I used to love helping to wind the wool into balls, but I didn't much care for it when new wool was purchased, for it came in hanks and you had to stand with your arms apart, hands stiff, supporting the wool on your wrists, while someone else rolled it up. There was a neat little wrist action that allowed the last few strands to slip off neatly without catching on your thumbs. But your arms got very tired holding it, and as we did a lot of hand-knitting – Mona even knitted suits for my teddy bear – my mother hit upon the idea of stretching the hanks across the back of a kitchen chair. It was just the right height and width, and everyone's arms were the better for it.

Anything past wearing or altering might have its zip fastener removed, its hooks and eyes snipped off, before being cut up for dusters or floor cloths. Anybody buying cleaning cloths would have been considered only fit for 'the big house' in Omagh. I was man-big before I bought my first bundle of yellow dusters on a stall in Cookstown. But best of all, we might save the buttons.

One of my most treasured memories is Granny Campbell's button box, originally, I suspect, a fancy tea caddy, possibly a Christmas present, before being recycled as a container for something quite other, and a source of constant fascination for a small girl. We never bought a button in our lives, for there was always something that would match (or nearly) in the casket, but to me it was far more than a box of fasteners. It was a treasure trove of exoticism, for among the ordinary white shirt buttons and run-of-the-mill coloured ones, there were the mother-of-pearl, the enamel, the brass, the embossed, even, though I did not know it then, Victorian and Edwardian wonders, for Granny had had some of these from her mother's time, and she herself was born in 1892. There were buttons made of glass, like miniature paper-weights; tiny pieces of jet that might have adorned a tea-gown; a buckle or two, and a gold dress clip, that we always meant to put on something else, but never got around to it. I still have it. There were buttons of all shapes and sizes, from cuff buttons to Chanel-style embellishments, and most wondrously, the odd square or triangular one. I was allowed to play with them if I was very careful, and many a story was woven around them to keep me occupied.

My grandmother made clothes for me when I was little, often lavishly embroidered for she was a remarkable needlewoman, and Mona, whom I always called 'Posy' for reasons that have completely escaped me now, was a first-class knitter, so we all wore gorgeous hand-knits. When it came to the finishing touch-es, there was always a length of lace or a bit of braid that could be re-used; but the *pièce de résistance* always came from the button box.

Another great pastime of my mum's which sometimes allowed her to recycle stuff was 'titivating'. Mona would have cleaned till the cows came home, but it was Maureen who papered, painted, draped curtains, slanted a photograph just so on a mantelpiece, or juxtaposed two unlikely pieces of furniture together. In pursuit of this hobby, she often mixed her own paint, sometimes with surprising results, such as when she painted the Sacred Heart altar purple. Wilf had built us some kitchen cupboards with pan-elled doors, and Granny used to say she was afraid to go out, for she never knew what colour the cabinets would be when she got back. They were a particular favourite because their design allowed Maureen to mix and match, so the sides and frame might be one colour, the door panels quite another.

The chimney breast was another favourite target, and it was the site for experiments with stippling, dragging, and distressing, long before these techniques became fashionable, and much loved of the TV makeover kids. One neighbour was much taken with the stippling and decided to have a go in her own house, but she didn't realise that you had to apply the stippling with an almost dry brush, over a quite dry ground. The resulting pastiche of base colour and asymmetric blobs with the excess paint running down the walls in rivulets was beyond dramatic.

Mum also loved the so-called contemporary look, in which opposite walls were papered in different but complementary designs, for then she could use up paper that was left over from another room, or even buy up odd rolls in Meenagh's, and if it didn't work there was a chance that you would only have to re-do two of the walls for the other two might be okay.

She loved distemper. The walls in our kitchen were not the smoothest and damp was a problem, so we decorated frequently, and distemper would give the place a quick face-lift until you could do things right. One night she was engaged on her frescoes when Gerald came in. She apologised for the state of the place, pointed out that she was busy, and hoped he would take the hint and go, but he did not. He took up position at the end of the table, the only piece of furniture still in its original location, and she had to work around him as best she might.

We had just acquired a new puppy, Sooty by name, a black and tan terrier possessed of more energy that any dog should ever have, and he was having a fine time investigating things he hadn't seen before, Gerald among them. The rest of the family were safely ensconced in the sitting room out of the way of Maureen, the paint pot, and the marauding pup, but Gerald stubbornly remained where he was despite the inconvenience to all concerned, and complained about the unruly behaviour of the dog.

"It's only a pup, Gerald." remarked my mother mildly, painting on.

"Nevertheless, Maureen, it is behaving in a most inconsiderate way."

She rolled the eyes. Wilf came in and stood for a minute by the fire watching the progress of the work as he demolished a Woodbine. The pup jumped up and grabbed Wilf's cap out of his pocket, making a dash for cover, then creeping out just enough to identify its hiding place and initiate a chivvy. Gerald was delighted. He would have an ally.

"Wilf! Wilf! The dog has seized your cap. After it! After it!" Wilf looked at him as if he was demented.

"Damn the bit of harm it'll do it," he said. "Here, pup, gimme that." In the way of all young things, the pup quickly lost interest.

It wasn't long before Mona descended the stairs to see if there was any chance of a drop of tea, with me paddling after her like her shadow. We found Gerald in a corner, behind a barricade constructed out of my toys: a pram, a tricycle, a scooter, several boxes, a doll's cot, that he had abstracted from the mousehouse, the name I gave to the cubby-hole under the stairs simply because we once caught a mouse there. They never knew that in later years we had another mouse in the sitting-room, whom I fed with crumbs saved from the table and named Sarsfield after one of my favourite characters from Ireland's romantic past. Eventually I guess he got too fat for the hole or someone else treated him less kindly, for one day he simply stopped coming.

"What in under God have you these here for, Maureen?" Mona wanted to know, glancing at the toys. She naturally assumed they had been piled up because of the re-decoration, and began to clear them. Mum replied evenly, never lifting her gaze,

"Oh, I didn't put them there. Gerald's afraid of the dog; he has those for protection."

In the same breath he was calling out to Mona not to remove them on any account. She regarded him with her level gaze, her beautiful eyes filled with a mixture of derision, incredulity and pure amusement.

"Are you telling me that you're afraid of *that?*" she asked pointing to the tiny morsel now hanging onto my hand. Gerald looked pained.

"It's vicious," he replied.

"Catch yourself on," she said, lifting the toys away. "Aideen, put these back where they belong."

Gerald was the picture of offended dignity. He turned to mum.

"Maureen, since your sister is so unsympathetic, I must insist that you give me a stick to hit the dog with if it comes near me. I really do believe it has ill intentions."

There was silence for all of five seconds. The Campbells' love of dogs runs very deep, is something intense and instinctive, and I have never in all my life seen a Campbell hit an animal. He might as well have suggested striking me. My mother turned to him, and in one of those moments in which the action seems to be slowed right down to allow you to savour every millisecond, solemnly took the stirring stick out of the pot of distemper and handed it to him, paint side first.

He grasped it without thinking, and the look on his face when he realised what he had done was quite something. Slowly he set the stick on the ground, pulled a handkerchief from his pocket and ostentatiously wiped his hands. He was furious. He turned again to Mona.

"This is intolerable. If you won't remove that mongrel I will have to go. Quite simply, it's either me or the dog!"

Mona gave him one of the dazzling smiles that made many an admirer go weak at the knees.

"In that case, Gerald," she purred at him, "it's the dog."

He gathered his dignity about him as best he could, and headed for the stairs. With a last disdainful look over his shoulder he placed one foot on the bottom step and the other on the dog's ball. His exit was somewhat spoiled by the unintentional stumble up at least four steps and the painful crack to the shins from the resulting fall.

Many of the great culinary stand-byes of my childhood were devised as ways of using up leftovers, and now they regularly appear on the menus of fancy 'ating-houses. Who would have thought that champ would suddenly become exotic? Or that you would add parsnips to it? And what about shepherd's pie, or bread and butter pudding? And it's not the first time I've heard the comment, "This milk's turned, I'll have to make pancakes"; or sat down to a bowl of panada, where the stale bread would be sweetened with plenty of sugar before being soaked in tea and served in a bowl like a soup. And if you've never eaten panada, you don't know what you're missing. There was also my favourite nursery trifle, which while not exactly designed for leftovers could nonetheless be prepared if the sponges were slightly stale. To make it, you crumbled up a few trifle sponges, added a small tin of fruit cocktail, and sloshed in a generous measure of brown lemonade. We never called it red lemonade! The longer it sat, the nicer it got. A friend made this concoction for me a few years ago when I came out of hospital, and it tasted like manna, or at least my idea of manna. This may have been because post-operatively I was in need of some TLC, or because the hospital food was inedible to the point of being life-threatening. Or could it have been that with every spoonful I tasted my youth again? Why quibble? It was delicious.

My mother would be horrified at the amount of food that we waste nowadays, for besides being threatened with the hungry crows, I was often warned that (a) I might be reduced to gathering stones as a punishment for wasting food; or (b) the starving children in Biafra would be glad of it.

Many of the neighbours I knew kept a few hens, and they got the bread that was beyond culinary redemption. We had one recycler who made it her business to go around the houses col-

———— ∞ ————

lecting scraps for the hens and pigs. Aggie was well known to everybody. Once a week the front door would open and a clarion call would float down into the basement kitchen:

"Ha' ye any brock?"

Aggie wasn't overly endowed with intellectual prowess, and many and varied were the descriptions used to indicate this state of affairs: 'there's a wee want', 'her head's cut,' 'she's not the full shilling', or 'the lights are on but there's nobody at home'. My mother once had the privilege of giving her a Marcel wave. Aggie was delighted with the result, not surprisingly since her natural look resembled a pea's wisp. Several weeks later, she went missing. Rumours abounded as to where she might be, and the removal from the town of a regiment of soldiers was suggested as a possible reason for her decamping without forwarding address. Whatever the truth, eventually our front door opened one night and a familiar refrain rent the air:

"Ha' ye any brock?"

As my mother was handing over the bag of stale bread, she said,

"Welcome back, Aggie. Did you know there was an SOS out for you on the radio?"

Aggie beamed at her, totally unabashed.

"Did they say I had curly hair?" was all she wanted to know.

Hatch

Charlie Campbell

I was unique on the Donaghmore Road in being a cuckoo clutch. Every other family there and in Charlemont Street boasted at least four, sometimes more, children, often quite close in age. This meant that the mothers never had to hire help with baby-sitting, though God knows they needed it, for the older kids reared the younger ones, with only 'the baby' getting off with it. And me. I knew nothing about infants save that when you met a new-born being paraded by a fond parent it was customary to cross its palm with silver, and that my Uncle Charlie always followed his own advice if asked who he thought the child resembled.

"I always say the mother," he explained, "for it's usually the mother that's asking, and it pleases her. And it's safer, for at least you're always sure who the mother is."

The extended families also meant that there was a ready supply of participants for our games. And what games!

———— ∾ ————

Here we go round the mulberry bush, the mulberry bush,
the mulberry bush…

March the robbers coming through, coming through, coming
through, March the robbers coming through, my fair lady!

The farmer wants a wife, the farmer wants a wife,
Ee-ay-addio, the farmer wants a wife!

The incidental music of our youth. Who can forget those marvellous days of summer, when the sky was bluer, the sun was hotter, and the light lasted longer that at any time after you passed the age of ten? The Donaghmore Road rang to the sound of children's voices, and many's the day there would be several 'rings' going at once, the protagonists in each striving to outdo the others in volume if not in harmony. The best fun was when they all joined in and made the ring so big that it spilled out into the road, and we were very annoyed if a car appeared to spoil our activities, though this was a rare occurrence. If you didn't have enough kids gathered for a ring game you could try the bush telegraph:

Garry up, garry up for a big big ring!
If you don't come now, you'll not get in!

And when you got your crowd you had a choice of games: Dusty Bluebells; Tip-a-rip-a-rapper on the dead man's shoulder; In and out the windows; On yonder hill there stands a lady; or my favourite:

This is the way the teacher stands,
This is the way she folds her arms,
This is the way she claps her hands,
And this is the way she dances!

————

Green peas and barley-o, barley -o, barley-o,
Green peas and barley-o, sugar cane and candy.

A friend who grew up in Belfast always sang *sugar puffs and candy,* but in Dungannon we were still on the porridge.

If you tired of rings, there were always alternatives: What time is it, Mr. Wolf?; A-hunting we will go; Nuts in May; or Cat'n'bat. We played ring-a-rosie, and cared not one jot that it had its origins in a charm against bubonic plague; and Tig, with all the counting rhymes attached to it:

Eeney-meeney-miney-mo! Catch a nigger by the toe,
When he squeals, let him go, Eeney-meeney-miney-mo!

We had no idea how politically incorrect it was, would not have understood how anyone could be offended, but we preferred another version because we thought it naughty:

Eeney-meeney-miney-mo! Set the baby on the po!
When he's done, clean his bum, Eeney-meeney-miney-mo!

Do you remember *One two sky blue all out but you!* Or *Eenta meenta mackeracka, ray-a-ro domino, arraballa cubanalla, Mackintosh's toffee-o!* Our first experience of gobbledy-gook and we didn't know it. There were rhymes for everything, and for many this was our earliest acquaintance with poetry and music, as we absorbed the idea of cadence, metre, and rhythm without anyone noticing. There was one game, taught me by my friend Marian, that involved two lines of kids dancing up and down towards and then away from each other and singing in turn:

What are you riding here for, here for, here for?
What are you riding here for, Y - O - U!

I'm riding here to get married, married, married,
I'm riding here to get married, Y - O - U!

Will you marry me sir, me sir, me sir?
Will you marry me sir, Y - O - U!

You're too black and dirty, dirty, dirty,
You're too black and dirty, Y - O - U!

Well you're as black as a poker, a poker, a poker,
You're as black as a poker, Y - O - U!

In later years when I went to Dublin and learned to ceilidh dance, I could never get through *The Waves of Tory* without fighting the temptation to launch into this chant! See what memories these rhymes evoke for you:

Cinderella dressed in yella went upstairs to meet her fella,
How many kisses did she give him? One… two… three…

Vote vote vote for Aideen D'Arcy, in comes Annie at the door,
Annie is the one who will have a bit of fun,
So we don't want Aideen any more.

The maid was in the kitchen doing a bit of stitching,
In jumped the beggar man and out jumped she!

All in together this fine weather,
Whoever chucks the rope has to take an end.
Shoot, fire, gun, run, nineteen twenty leave the rope empty!

A tinker, a tailor, a soldier, a sailor,
Rich man, poor man, beggar man, thief!

Mercenary little brutes that we were, we didn't mind *beggar man* or *thief* because they were unlikely to come within our orbit, but we hated to chuck the rope on *poor man!*

Eileen Conlon, dark and pretty with porcelain complexion, and a few years older than me, taught me to skip. I had a proper rope with wooden handles painted in bright colours but try as I might I couldn't get the rhythm going, and wound up every time with my feet in a knot. I came into our house howling with rage and frustration, only to be sent back out to try again, with one of my mother's favourite mantras ringing in my ears: *Many men fail because they fail to try.* I was unimpressed, because I knew fine rightly that everyone could skip as soon as they picked up a rope, except for me. But Eileen persevered, and I persevered, and all of a sudden, the miracle happened: the rope, my arms, and my feet all found the rhythm at the same time and I was off! I could skip on the spot, I could skip across the backs, I could skip backwards, I could skip with my arms crossed, I could even – oh joy! – jump into a long turning rope *lap of the moon,* and that wasn't easy! Soon the smart rope was abandoned in favour of the communal one that somebody's father brought home from work, for there was always more fun when you had a crowd. Eileen often made one of us, until, in her early teens, she was struck down by a crippling illness that I believe to have been a form of arthritis. The last time I saw her she was confined to a wheelchair, still dark, still pretty, but no longer teaching anyone to skip.

It makes me tired just to think of it today, but I wonder if we would have such startling statistics of child obesity if we threw out a few computers and Gameboys and let the kids loose with a rope, a bat, and a ball. None of my friends carried excess weight, though to be fair we wouldn't have thought anything of it if they had, for we were lucky enough not to be obsessed with image. We were all relentlessly fit, and gorged on fresh air. The only thing that curtailed our playtime was the call *"You're a-lukkin'"* or the fall of another dusky evening.

Indoors the fun continued. I remember Aunt Mona sitting with legs crossed on a low chair, with me astride her ankle, facing her, holding onto her two hands while she danced me up and down and sang *Yip wee horsey go for sand, all the way to Killyman!* She might as well have said Killimanjaro, so exotic did it sound to my two-year-old ears. Tents were made from sheets strung between chairs, a Lloyd Loom bedroom chair was turned upside down to emulate a coach fit for a princess, and board games were common in every house: ludo, snakes and ladders, tiddlywinks, and Monopoly and Cluedo as you grew older. In our house we played cards, and at nine I was a master of Dan McGrew's favourite game, Solo. Wilf taught me Twenty-five, Daddy taught me Poker, but Mona taught me Switch which was better than any.

Many children have an imaginary friend but I had to go one better – I had an alter ego called Mrs. Feeney, who had several children, notably Brian and Rosabelle, and while mostly I transmuted into Mrs., I did, on the rare occasion, deign to become Rosabelle. Never Brian! Mrs. Feeney had a whole life system attached to her. I knew where she lived, what her husband did, what she cooked for dinner, and that she had a little shop where she worked when the notion took her. It was a drapery of sorts, or a haberdashery, for it was stocked by the masses of handkerchiefs I received for every birthday, Christmas, and Easter, most of which were never taken out of their boxes. We had hundreds of them. There were fine linen ones with filigree hemstitching, white cotton with embroidered corners, pale pastels with scalloped edges, curiosities from Great-Aunt Lil in London like the two gingham ones folded to look like a pair of bloomers. They came in tartan, candy-stripe, polka dot, and shower of hail, trimmed with ribbons and tiny bows. They came in boxes, packages, tissue paper and cellophane. They came singly, in pairs, in sets of four, and occasionally in a long box with one for every day of the week; and they came in very handy when I wanted to turn the corner of our sitting room into my wee shop. It helped that I had an aunt who enjoyed make-believe as much as I did, or so it appeared to me at the time, for she acted out the parts of my many customers, from the farmer's wife who was a bit of a gipe to the school teacher who was hard to please, or the local gossip, Mrs. Garrity, with a sharp word to say about all the others. She played them all, each *dramatis persona* having a name and a specific identity. And she never mixed them up.

Children were valued when I was a kid, though not above their station. You never knew whose progeny you might be feeding and I have eaten boiled eggs the length and breadth of the Donaghmore Road and loathed them all, but you ate what was put in front of you without complaint, especially in someone else's house. Kids were never allowed to assume centre stage. It wasn't quite a case of being seen but not heard, and I have wonderful memories of the games played around the fire, but when adults came in you were sent off with a book or a toy, inside if it was raining, outside if it was fine.

Mind you, there was often just cause for such precautionary measures. Granny Campbell, usually more alert, dropped a word one night in front of the boy Wilf.

"I hope that Miss McCann doesn't stay long. Maybe if I don't make her tea, she'll go early."

This was very unusual for my grandmother, but Miss McCann used to deliver tracts and improving literature, then spend the evening admonishing wickedness and advising everyone present on how they could improve their lives, and Granny had had enough. My family loved visitors, but more especially, they loved crack.

In God's good time the lady came, spoke, lectured, and finally got up to go. Things went according to plan until she got halfway to the front door. Then she remembered she had not specifically said good night to Wilf, who was about six at the time. She turned.

"Good night, Wilfred son," she amended. Wilf beamed.

"Good night, Miss McCann. Peace be after you, Miss McCann. You got no tea the night, Miss McCann. My mother said she would make you none, and she didn't, Miss McCann. See you next week, Miss McCann…"

Needless to say, he didn't. In fact, we never had the pleasure of a visit from her again. I have often wondered why.

John was another who tended to think everyone doomed to damnation except himself. He was in our house one night before my mum was due to go to Birmingham for a few weeks' holiday. My great-aunt Monica was in the company too, and she listened a while in amazement as John held forth on the evils of this city, the areas to be avoided, the dens of iniquity that were springing up on every corner, the snares lying in the path of the innocent and foolish, till you would have been forgiven for thinking that God had made a serious miscalculation in destroying Sodom and Gomorrah and leaving Birmingham standing. Finally Monica asked a question.

"I wonder, John, just how it is that you seem to know so much about these situations and locales that the rest of us have never encountered?"

"I better get on home," he said, with unwonted enthusiasm.

Match

Mo Campbell

Marry in haste, repent at leisure, they say, and it was a foolish girl indeed who did not take heed of the numerous tips available to ensure she made the right decision regarding not just her choice of husband but the arrangements for the big day itself. Mind you, our friend Christie used to remark that 'The say would drown ye,' but that's another story.

Weddings had to be carefully planned, for the day, the time of year, the colour of the bride's outfit at a time when it was not *de rigueur* to wear white, were all governed by some hex or custom. My mother was well acquainted with such beliefs, and loved to recite the old rhymes connected with them.

There was a rhyme to help you choose the day, which went as follows:

Monday for health
Tuesday for wealth
Wednesday best day of all;

———— ∽ ————

Thursday for losses,
Friday for crosses,
Saturday no day at all!

She herself chose the last Wednesday in July, which in 1953 was the 29th, and was delighted to discover that it was also the feast day of Saint Martha, her favourite saint (and my patron), and I was born on a Wednesday, but for birthdays, of course, it's not such a hot number!

In terms of clothes, too, there was a rhyme to advise you of what to wear, or what not to wear. No need of Trinny and Susannah in those days!

Married in white, you have chosen all right,
Married in green, ashamed to be seen,
Married in grey, you will go far away,
Married in red, you will wish yourself dead,
Married in blue, love ever true,
Married in yellow, ashamed of your fellow,
Married in black, you will wish yourself back,
Married in pink, your spirits will sink,
Married in brown, you will live out of town,
Married in pearl, you will live in a whirl.

Of course, you could never tell who you might fall in love with, but it was considered unlucky if the prospective couple's surnames had the same initial:

Change the name but not the letter,
Marry for worse and not for better!

On the other hand, a woman who married a man whose surname was the same as her maiden name, was believed to acquire a cure for the whooping cough. To administer the cure, she was required to give the sufferer something made up of three elements, say a cup of tea with milk and sugar, or a slice of bread, butter, and jam.

Cats had an odd place in Irish households, not just where weddings were concerned. In the days when the customary greeting upon entering a house was "God save all here!", it was subject to an amendment if there was a feline about the place: "God save all here, except the cat!" It was widely believed that the neighbourhood cats met up at night to spread the gossip they had been listening to all day, so a careful household would never tell anything secret if the cat was within earshot. A bride on her wedding morning would take care to feed the cat early, for if it was offended, it might bring on a shower of rain!

Apart from the Hallowe'en rituals relating to courtship and marriage, there were other ways to get a hint of what your future spouse might look like. There was always great demand for a bit of bride's cake, not to eat but to put under the pillow of an unmarried girl to encourage dreams of her husband to be, and there was also a belief that the yarrow plant held the secret. In order to persuade it to share the knowledge, again in dreams, you had to dance around it and sing:

> *Yarrow, fair yarrow good morrow,*
> *And thrice good morrow to thee!*
> *I hope that by this time tomorrow*
> *You'll say who my true love shall be.*

Choosing a partner for life is an important decision, and a girl had to be careful. Walking out with a prospective beau for a few months might give you a good idea of his temperament, for you didn't want a man who hung his fiddle at the door: street angel, house divil. Meanness was to be guarded against, and a friend of my mother's told her she knew it was time for 'the big E' when her escort turned to her as they stood in the queue for the pictures and said,

———— ∞ ————

"Givvus your money now, for I don't like to see a girl paying for herself."

All women enjoy a bit of romance, and who could blame a girl if she declined a proposal such as "Wud you like to throw yer oul' shoes under my bed?" or worse still, "How wud you like to be buried with my people?"

You might have been forewarned that something like this would follow if you had received the invitation my mother once got at a dance in St. Patrick's Hall: "Can I borrow your chassis for a struggle?" And if you thought romance was dead there was the man who gave his sweetheart a squeeze and asked her lovingly, "Can I have a wee feel?" only to be advised, "Wait till me Da dies and we can have the whole farm."

But the prize for gallantry must go, I think, to the Carrickmore farmer who asked my cousin Mo to dance one night at a shindig in The Gap ballroom. After a few minutes he told her that she was a right wee girl and he wouldn't mind dancing her again.

"You're a quare sight better than the last cutty I had," he told her, "for no harm til her, but she was like my ass with false teeth."

Not that I want to cast aspersions on Carrickmore, another part of God's own county, for it was widely rumoured in Dungannon when I was small that there was a man there who had discovered a cure for which there was no known disease.

Mo has fond memories of the bus journey up to the remoter parts of Tyrone for the dances when she stayed with us as a teenager. There they all were, drenched in cheap perfume (her favourite was Freesia), smoking frenetically in a race to see who could get lung cancer first, done up to the nines and admiring each other's dresses, hairdos, or new shoes, and ignoring the routine stoning of the bus as it negotiated certain areas. The driver would mutter, "Hell roast them wee skitters," while the flotilla of butterflies aboard gaily disregarded any such interruption as irrelevant to the purpose of the trip, which was to have fun. Arrived home, mum or Mona would ask,

———————

—— ∞ ——

"Did you have a good night?"

"Great, the band was fab."

"Did you click?"

"Only my heels."

"I suppose the bus was stoned?"

"Oh, yeah."

"Aye, as usual. Do you want a cup of tea?"

For young women heading out on a date there was plenty of advice, if they had wanted to take it, but none so succinct as that offered by a lady who, again, was lodging with one of the families on the Donaghmore Road. The lady's name I don't know, so I'll call her Sara, but the daughter was called Milizzie. To my mum and her pals they seemed rustic and a bit green, and the fact that Milizzie had even got a date was wonderful in itself, for in mum's estimation she was 'a cure for bad thoughts', but there's no accounting for taste. We all know that God never made an oul' shoe but He made an oul' sock. Milizzie and her beau were to meet the next night at eight, and Sara spent the evening discussing preparations with her offspring, interspersing the diatribe with, "Now remember, Milizzie, don't allow him to get bold."

Gogga Rice reported to mum the following evening that she had observed Milizzie flying up Anne Street, along the Donaghmore Road, and into the house as if the Furies were after her. Gogga followed her in, eager for a full report. She was just in time to catch Sara's anguished question,

"What's wrong, Milizzie daughter, that you're back so early?" and Milizzie's reply: "Och, Ma! He was just beginning to get bold!"

My mother's attitude to the superstitions that governed all forms of daily activity, not just those associated with courtship and marriage, was somewhat ambivalent. She enjoyed collecting them, the more absurd the better, and some were treated with a good deal of scepticism. She thought it crazy not to walk under a ladder, had no qualms about doing anything on Friday 13th, and attached no importance to black cats; but others she was watchful about. I think her sensible head told her that most of them were nonsense, but another, more atavistic, sense reminded her that we belong to a very ancient race who understood the earth and all its mysteries a whole lot better than we do, and she recognised that some beliefs that had degenerated into old wives' tales might have started out with a firm foundation in something a lot more important. There were certain customs that she honoured to the day she died, and if she believed in some of them, I suspect she just took the crack out of the others!

She hated to see anyone spill salt, saying 'spill salt, spill tears', and she immediately made you cast a drop over your left shoulder to hit the Devil in the eye. She objected to anyone singing at the table, warning, 'If you sing at your meals, there'll be tears at your heels', though that might just have been her way of putting manners on us. She always took the Christmas decorations down before Twelfth Night, she wouldn't allow anyone to meet or pass her on the stairs, and she steadfastly refused to take the third light from a match, in the days when everyone smoked. I read somewhere that this custom stemmed from the days of trench warfare. If there was a sniper about, he would be alerted by the first flare of the match, draw a bead on the second, and follow through on the third with a perfect target, meaning that the third smoker would be hit, but I'm sure my mum knew nothing about that, any more than she knew that salt used to be regarded as a very valuable commodity and Roman soldiers received a portion of their pay in salt, thus giving us the word *salary*.

She detested anyone putting new shoes on the table, and always said that if you accidentally put a garment on inside out, it was a sign of good luck coming your way. Similarly, it was lucky to find a pin on the floor but only if you picked it up, for 'see a pin and pick it up, all that day you'll have good luck; see a pin and let it lie, then that day you're sure to cry.'

She would never allow me to cut my nails on a Sunday, warning me 'Friday cut hair, Sunday cut horn, better for you that you'd never been born!' The argument that my nails were *nails* and not, in fact, *horn,* had no influence with her. But she allowed that it was lucky to wash your hair on Good Friday! She liked it when something good happened on a Monday, saying 'Good Monday, good week', but didn't subscribe to the common belief that it was unlucky to sew or knit on Sunday, undeterred by the threat that you would have to rip it out with your nose when you got to Heaven. As our friend Annie Convery said, "Aren't you better doing a wee bit of needlework than sitting thinking oul bad thoughts?" I don't imagine Annie ever had a bad thought in her life.

The fire was alive with symbolism, a relic no doubt from our Celtic forbears, who lived in dread of the fire in the homestead going out. This is why the fire was always banked at night but never extinguished, so that it could be blown into new life again each morning. It was a symbol of life itself, and it provided a means of heating and cooking, a source of light, and it kept predators at bay, as well as serving as a sign of welcome. A young woman who could make a good fire was sure to get a good-hearted husband; the fire burning to one side was the sign of a parting; a blue flame meant frost was on the way, while a film of coal flapping on the bars of the grate heralded a visitor. To find out which day he might come, you had to clap your hands in front of it and recite the days of the week, beginning with the following one. When the film flew off, that was the day your visitor would arrive. And if a piece of coal flew out at someone, they were in for a windfall of money.

Anyone giving fire out of the house on a May Eve, even to the extent of giving a passing traveller a light for his pipe, was running a high risk of letting the fairies in on them, but if you put mayflowers out around all the portals to the house, window sills, door steps and so on, then you could thwart their evil designs. This was especially important if you had a young baby in the house, for you didn't want to wake up next day and find that a changeling or fairy substitute had been left in place of the stolen child. The fairies are said to love and cherish the baby thus

———— ∞ ————

taken for since they are immortal they don't have babes of their own, but this is small consolation for the mother, who is left with either an aged and crabbed goblin, whose sole purpose in life appears to be to work mischief, probably as a result of being turfed out in favour of a human child, or else a simulacrum of the baby which will fade and wither as the year progresses, being gone by the autumn.

Parts of the body could indicate imminent happenings too. If the sole of the foot itched, you were going to be on strange ground, if your right palm itched, you would be introduced to someone new, but if it was the left palm, there was money coming to you. We all know about itchy ears, of course. If your ears itch, someone is talking about you – left for love, right for spite, reverse at night!

Mum had an odd custom that I've only ever seen practised in my family so I have no idea of its provenance. If two of us inadvertently spoke in the same breath saying exactly the same words, say both looking up together and saying "Is that the time?", we would immediately link the little fingers of our right hands together and make a wish, without breaking the silence. After a couple of seconds, we would twist our hands until our thumbs were touching, release the little fingers, and shake hands. One person would then say the name of the first poet to come into their head, and the other would respond with a different one. Crazy? Quite possibly, but sure, who knows?

In Two Minds

She said: I love you.

Just one glimpse of your face and my spirit takes wing,
When you speak I hear music; you smile and I sing;
Like a falcon released from the hunter's restraint
I soar till I'm breathless; we kiss, and I'm faint.
My heart skips a beat when you reach for my hand,
It pounds like a drum in a military band;
My pulse rate goes up, my defences go down,
I'd follow you barefoot from country to town.
The moment our eyes met, I knew I was lost,
I'm yours without question, not counting the cost...

And he said: Great! Now, I love you too.

You're a slick raconteur, the perfect hostess,
You're elegant, stylish, you dress to impress.
Every head turns when you enter a room
With a whisper of silk, on a waft of perfume.
I've seen my friends stare when we're out on the tiles –
We make quite a couple, we doyens of style!
You're chic, you're soignée, you're the cream of your sex,
An excellent wife for a smart young exec.
With me as the captain and you as the crew
They'll be pea-green with envy at all I can do!
There's simply no telling how far I could go!

My dear, will you marry me?

And she said: Oh No!

Dispatch

Una and Shona Campbell

Sarah Gallogly was a-waitin' on. Having no close relatives nearby save an elderly sister, Teenie, it fell to the neighbours to sit up with her. Johnny Murphy had done it the night before, accompanied by his wife Mamie and her sister Susie Campbell, but tonight it was the turn of my Uncle Wilf and the other two Campbells of Charlemont Street – Una and Shona. This was a duty that often fell to Wilf, and I can only guess at the reason. My family was famous for sitting up late, and he was known as a man of steel nerve whom you could trust anywhere, so he seemed a likely candidate. Having done it once, you make a stick for your own back. He was also the one who went to funerals, for at that time, though the women might go to the funeral Mass, it was only the men who walked to the graveside, while the women went on home to get the sandwiches ready. One time there had been a spate of deaths in and around the Donaghmore Road and my mother, being the sociable one, was getting ready to head out to another wake.

—— ✎ ——

"Do you know," she sighed, tying on the turban, "I'm sick, sore, and tired, of going to wakes."

Granny looked up from her embroidery. "And I'm broke buying Mass cards."

Wilf lit another Woodbine. "It's all right for you," he complained, "but I'm near dead meself walking after funerals."

The vigil in Gallogly's took place in a small upstairs parlour, with Sarah's bedroom off it. Una decided to lead the company in a recital of the Rosary, and Wilf being hard of hearing had them all in stitches with his delayed and often inappropriate responses. When Una announced, "Thou, oh Lord, shalt open my lips," he turned to her with a bewildered look on his face and said "Pardon?" as if he hadn't a clue what she was talking about. At a distance of years, I'd wager that only half of his misunderstanding was genuine.

In the wee small hours of the morning, Una, who was terrified of anything to do with death and was only there out of the goodness of her nature, crouched over the tiny fire that was surviving against the odds in the grate.

"Wilf," says she, "Should we not open the window a wee bit? They say the soul goes out through the window, and Sarah's very low."

"Och, catch yerself on, Una daughter," Wilf reassured her. "It's up the chimney it goes."

Wilf later declared that he had never seen Una move so fast.

The same night, the water was turned off in the town to allow some essential repairs to be carried out, and Una was gasping for a cup of tea. Teenie assured her that she had saved a kettleful for just such an emergency, and she would go at once and brew up. Una's face said it all. Teenie's standards of hygiene did not measure up to Una's, and she did not relish drinking anything that the old lady might prepare, but she was much too polite to say so. This was where Wilf came in handy.

"Sit there, Teenie ye girl ye, and I'll make it." He departed to the kitchen, resolutely refusing to catch Una's eye, as she strove desperately to indicate that she had suddenly lost her taste for it. A moment later he was back.

"Teenie, daughter, you must have forgot to fill the kettle; there's not a drop in it."

"Are you sure, son?" Teenie bustled out to check.

"I'm sure, right enough," Wilf said to her departing back, then, turning to Una, "for I poured it down the sink meself."

The next day being Sunday they decided to go to the half-six Mass before going home to bed. As they entered the chapel it occurred to Una that Wilf mightn't want to go right up the aisle for like most men he usually stood at the back. In deference to this, she selected a pew about three or four from the last. Half way through the service he nudged her.

"I've nivver been as far up the chapel in me life."

She was lucky not to have been with my great-uncle Tom. He walked into the chapel one Sunday and selected a pew, at the end of which sat Nellie, notorious for refusing to move up or to allow anyone to get past her, no matter how little space there was elsewhere. Tom stood ostentatiously for a moment but Nellie stayed where she was. As he moved on, he favoured her with a sardonic glance before announcing in ringing tones,

"I presume you've bought it!"

When Sarah finally died the corpse was washed and laid out ready for coffining. After some discussion and a fair bit of head-shaking, Wilf was called upon for advice as to how they might get the coffin down the stairs, for the Charlemont houses were narrow, the stairs steep. He weighed up the situation and finally called on the assistance of a neighbour man who was of a respectable height.

"We'll have to lower it over the banister," he explained, "for it'll never turn the corner with the body in it, the more wee Sarah's not too heavy. You stand in the hallway with your arms up and take the weight to balance it, and two of us will lower it down to you. Then a couple more will steady it and get it into the hearse."

Half an hour later Wilf came downstairs to find your man on duty in the hallway with his arms at full stretch above his head, looking a trifle pained but giving Casabianca a run for his money.

"What are you doing?" asked Wilf.

"Waiting for the coffin," was the reply.

Wilf looked at him as if he had just sprouted horns.

"Och, Jaysus, man, you'll have some wait. We're not taking the coffin down till the morra morning!"

The friendship between the two Campbell families went back farther than I can remember, probably to the days when my folks lived for a spell in Charlemont Street, before moving up the hill to the Donaghmore Road. It was one of those friendships than spanned all the age ranges: Mona and wee Una were pals, as were mum and Shona; my Uncle Charlie was great with their brother John.

The milkman on the Donaghmore Road was Joe McStravick, and he took immense delight in telling Mona, then a mere teenager, that he would marry her as soon as she was old enough. This incensed her, for although he was probably a man in his prime she thought him ancient, and it didn't help that Charlie and John used to sit in our front room when she was out of sight but within earshot and act out the part of two old fellows looking back on their lives.

"What ever became of oul Mona?"

"Sure didn't she marry McStravick and have ten children."

Sadly neither John nor Charlie was destined to scratch a grey head. Hodgkin's disease claimed Charlie's life when he was barely fifty, but John died in his early twenties, a victim, I think, of TB, which was still a killer to be feared. As he lay dying, Una was dispatched to fetch Charlie from the shop in Irish Street where he worked. He got home in time to see John open his eyes wide in wonderment and say,

"I think I see a shower of beautiful white confetti," as he gently slipped away.

It used to be customary to stop the clocks when someone died, to cover the mirrors lest the soul of the dead person become trapped within the glass, there to remain until the last trump; to muffle the door knocker, and pull down the blinds. Most people died at home because hospital really was a last resort, and wakes were showcases for the very best in community spirit. In the days when no one had washing machines, Mrs. Conlon took the bed linen from our house wherein mum and Mona nursed Granny Campbell for three months before her death, washed it all by hand, and brought it back ironed to perfection. Neighbour women made copious amounts of tea, neighbour men might bring in a few drinks. A friend of mine went to a wake in the country of an elderly man who was survived by two equally elderly brothers. As the night wore on, one of these pulled from under the bed, where the remains was laid out, a crateful of bottles of Guinness, thick with dust. He gave each a cursory wipe on his sleeve before opening it with an old pen-knife, and solemnly handing one to every man there.

"We were keeping these for the wake," he told them. He didn't say for how long. In Tyrone it would have been considered polite to give the corpse – if male – a bottle too, and even to deal him a hand of cards, because it would not do for the dead person to think himself so soon forgotten by his peers.

At my great-grandfather's wake in Ballymulderg they quickly ran out of seats, for country wakes are huge. The men from the local Orange lodge went up to the hall and brought down every chair and bench they could carry, left them there until after the funeral, then collected them and brought them back.

I was eight when Granny Campbell died. The night before, the banshee, who, they say, follows the Mac's and the O's[4], howled three times in the back garden, waking Teesie Ritchie and Billy, and the dog Sooty refused to come into the house, maintaining a lonely vigil in the back hall. I was taken in to a neighbour's

---

[4] Granny Campbell's maiden name was O Lorcain in the original Irish

house, cossetted and amused until all the necessary details had been attended to, before being sent back next morning, bathed, dressed, and fed. I ate a boiled egg, something I would never do at home, with great relish, and sat beside Willie John, said to be an odd man, while he shaved at the sink in the basement kitchen, all the while chatting to me and telling me stories.

The day after the burial, McGearys opened their house to the extended family group who were over for the funeral, and cooked us a delicious lunch. Seamus O'Neill handed my Uncle Charlie the keys of his car, a rare luxury in those days, and said, "My car is at your disposal while you're here."

One of those who came to the wake was Lizzie O'Neill, a woman about whom I knew nothing more than that she was a witch and therefore to be avoided at all costs. My Uncle Charlie, who knew better, handed her a wee whiskey as soon as she sat down. Her tongue loosened after it, and maybe another one, she treated us to reminiscences of her youth.

"I mightn't be much to look at now," she told us, "but when I was younger I was a fine girl, like a horse."

She could read tea leaves, and my mother's cousin, yet another Maureen, handed over her cup.

"I see you here," said Lizzie, "going down a long room and stopping every now and then to tend to something. But you haven't done this for a while." Maureen had been a nurse in the Mid-Ulster Hospital before her marriage.

"And I see you standing beside a coffin," she went on, "and maybe two. But neither one is the one you're here for tonight." Less than eight months later, her husband's brother and only sister died within six weeks of each other.

My family had no fear of death, believing that it was a gateway to a better world, and this conviction sustained them through many a loss. They could also find humour in every situation, it was their safety valve, and one of the funniest incidents occurred at my grandmother's funeral.

The undertaker, Peter, was a family friend, otherwise he would not have been chosen for the job, since it was generally agreed that he was about as much use as a trapdoor in a canoe. He arrived for the removal, and announced that he would say the Rosary. My mother said afterwards that she had never sat – or knelt – through anything like it. He pulled her down beside him at the bedside, muttering out of the corner of his mouth "Which Mysteries?" She told him *Sorrowful* was customary. He didn't know the sequence, but as each decade ended leant over to her and hissed in a stage whisper, "What's next?"; and instead of each decade having ten Hail Marys, some had five and some had fifteen.

When we got to the church, we found cousin Frances in the front pew wearing a huge pink picture hat adorned with flowers, but tried to ignore it. There had been a chimney fire in great-uncle Tom's house that morning, and as we waited for the church to fill up, Tom asked Peter if he would go and check that everything had now been safely dealt with.

"I will surely, Tom. Is it the chapel chimney?"

"Jesus Christ, man, no. The chimney in my house. Take a run up and just check that everything is sorted."

"Aye, all right. Will I take the hearse?" Tom silently handed him the keys of his own car.

When the cortège finally prepared to move off, Peter announced that he didn't know where he was going, for Granny was to be buried in Eglish graveyard, beyond The Loup, a small ancient cemetery in which most of the occupants are related to my grand-mother's family. It truly is God's Acre, one of those small enclaves forgotten by time and progress, nowadays marked with a green and white sign to denote a place of historical interest, if marked at all. There was talk of discontinuing interments there because no one had been buried in it for a number of years, and then my great-grandfather died. It was said that his funeral helped to re-establish the right of way, thereby ensuring that the place remained in use for years to come, so it seems fitting that my grandmother was one of the last to be buried there.

Peter would never have found it in a million years, so my mother advised him to ask Frances for directions, since she lived nearby, but he grabbed her by the arm and before she could say aye, naw, nor yes, installed her in the passenger seat of the hearse, so that she could guide him. I often wondered what on-coming motorists made of the pink-hatted vision leading a funeral procession, but sadly, I'll never know.

I do know that in later years when my Uncle Wilf had returned to Dungannon after twenty-six years in Birmingham, he expressed a wish to visit Eglish graveyard, so my friend Issy and I arranged to take him there. It was a gorgeous day. We visited several other places en route that we knew would be of interest to him, and we brought a picnic with us, including a flask of tea liberally laced with whiskey, a favourite beverage of his. Finally we pitched up at Eglish, where we found the burial place, but only after traversing a field full of curious bovines, and negotiating a path through the recent evidence of their occupation, with some difficulty in Wilf's case, for he was unsteady on the pins and carried a walking stick. The problem with Wilf and the stick was that he often forgot to use it for support and instead called upon it to reinforce some point the was making. After crossing a field full of cowpats you had to take evasive action if it swung too close to your head.

We examined the stones that remained, scraping off the accumulated detritus of decades, and pulling aside thick tendrils of ivy. We peeled away layers of moss, sorted out who was related to whom, and generally reflected on the transience of human existence and the vanity of all things mortal and material.

As we re-crossed the field, I slightly in front as trail-blazer, I was halted by a clarion call from my uncle. "Hi! Aideen! Aideen!"

I turned, "Yes, Wilf?"

He was beaming at me, leaning on the stick, with a reflective glow in his eyes.

"I'm just thinking…" I waited. "There's not many people having as good a day as us the day, now is there?"

Cobwebs and Countesses

Second from right, front row: A…i…d…e…n

"I got up this morning and made my beds, cleaned the windies, brushed the floors, and done down behind my pictures…" Mrs. Quinn, who lived at the top of Charlemont Street, was notoriously houseproud, and rumour had it, in the days when cobwebs were considered to be the best remedy for nosebleeds, that she dashed out of the house one day and ran up and down the street distractedly, asking if anybody had one they could lend her. And if you're wondering how you were supposed to apply such a cure, don't bother; I've been puzzling about it for years without working it out, so you might as well give up and read on.

She had a habit of apologising to all her callers for the state of the place, which was always pristine, but perhaps she needed the ratification which came from the inevitable response:

"But you have everything lovely."

One day she tried the ruse on Teesie Ritchie. Teesie glanced critically around the sitting room.

—— ∞ ——

"Sure a wee flick with the duster and a run round with the brush and it'll be grand."

It was Mrs. Quinn who invited Granny Campbell to accompany her to a wake, not long after Granny had moved into Dungannon. Granny declined, saying that she didn't know the family.

"Och sure, Mrs. Campbell, neither do I. I just want to get a look round the house."

But she had a kindly side, as most people do, and she also had a telephone, and it was to her house that the momentous news was relayed on the evening of July 14th 1954, when my Uncle Charlie rang from Birmingham to say that my mother had been delivered of a five-pound baby girl, and it was Uncle Wilf who took the call.

Mum enjoyed a chat with Teesie better than anyone, for she was fiercely intelligent, enjoying subtlety and the idiosyncrasies of human nature. Uncle Wilf had an acquaintance called John who drank with him in Daly's pub, and both enjoyed reading Westerns. Wilf read voraciously and always used to pass on any books he was finished with. If he got one with a lurid cover, especially if it showed a saloon girl displaying some décolletage, he made a great show of presenting it in a clandestine manner, telling John it was a 'bad book', and on no account must he allow Mrs. Daly to see it. She of course was in on the joke, unbeknownst to John, and always came along at the critical moment saying in icy tones, "What's that you're doing there?"

There would be great fluster and bluster as John secreted the offending item in the inside pocket of his overcoat, a procedure that would be repeated all over again when he returned the book to its owner. "That's a shocker, a shocker, boy. Don't let Mrs. Daly see that one."

"I'm damned if I know what John reads into them books," Wilf said once, in great bewilderment. "There's damn all in them."

And it was true, for this was well before J T Edson started to put sex into the old West, and it was rare to find a female mentioned in the tales, never mind in a salacious or titillating way. The mind is its own place, no mistake about it, and in case there should be any doubt as to the unusual capacity of John's, witness his failsafe scheme for making money. He would go to London, he reckoned, and meet up with some rich widow or better still, a wealthy spinster, and with a bit of flattery, get her to fall for his charms. He was a bit hazy on the detail, but the clincher was that he would lure her into his coils by telling her he was the Earl of Tyrone, and offering her the chance to become Countess, for rich ladies of a certain age were, he knew, bound to covet a title. At some stage he would get his hands on her money, but it wasn't altogether clear if this would be after he had brought her home to the less than stately pile he shared with his wife and numerous kids, or some time before he was forced to take the final step; but the ultimate plan was to leave her high, dry, and broken-hearted, and run off with the cash. He was absolutely serious about the plan, and spent many a night discussing it with the boys in Daly's, finally acknowledging that maybe he had left it a bit late, but if only he were a young fellow like Wilf there…

My mother told Teesie the yarn and she loved it. Several days later I was out playing with John's daughter, Dinah. We wandered off, as kids do, and when mum came in search of me, the birds had flown.

"Teesie!" she called over the fence. "Have you seen Aideen anywhere?"

"I have," Teesie responded, deadly serious. "She's away over the back with Lady Dinah."

Dinah was allowed to come and play in my house, and one night – I guess we were about four years old at the time – we were busily engaged in writing our names on large sheets of paper, perched at the kitchen table, clutching our thick crayons like grim death. A cry went up from Dinah.

"Mona! Your Aideen's stupid! She can't write her own name!"

I was protesting vigorously, and Mona knew that I could, so she came to investigate.

———— ∞ ————

"Show her! Show her!" gloated the Ivy League student, so I wrote my name, laboriously enough, I suppose, as kids do, but I did it correctly: A…i…d…e…e…n. "Now!" Dinah shrieked in triumph. "You see!"

Mona was genuinely puzzled. "But that's right, Dinah," she said. "A…i…d…e…e…n."

Dinah was doubled up with glee. "Oh, you're stupid too, Mona Campbell! You can't spell it either!"

Totally baffled, Mona had me do the task again, with Dinah pointing dementedly at the page. "There! There! Now do you see?" Mona had to admit defeat. "No, show me."

Dinah was only too glad to oblige. The problem, it emerged, was that I didn't dot the 'i' until I had finished writing the whole name, and in her opinion, it must be dotted as soon as it was written, otherwise it constituted a misspelling. Mona wisely refrained from argument, for was this not the girl who had sparked off a debate when she told us, on the 5th March, that it was her birthday the following day? "That's great, Dinah. Happy Birthday," said Mona. "So, you're a March baby."

"What do you mean?" she asked suspiciously.

"I mean you were born in March," Mona explained. Dinah went into peals of laughter.

"You are so stupid, Mona Campbell!" she crowed.

Mona was used to this accusation so it bothered her not at all, but again, she was puzzled.

"But I thought you said it was your birthday tomorrow?"

"So it is."

"Then you must have been born in March."

"You are so stupid! I was born up in my own house!"

Teesie told us that when she was a youngster her best pal had a baby brother whom she was allowed to take for walks in his pram. Teesie, having no younger siblings, thought this was quite the thing, and asked a neighbour woman if she could borrow her infant son Joe for an hour or two to take a dander out the road. The poor woman probably jumped at the chance of a few hours' respite, as off Teesie went, a spring in her step, and the baby in his high-perch perambulator.

As she walked along she began to study the child before her, and it occurred to her that she had never seen an uglier baby in her life. There was nothing of the bonny babe about him, no curls, no dimples, no limpid eyes, no coaxing smile, nothing. In fact, she told us, "he had a scrunched up ugly wee mug, all red and blotchy, with pop eyes, and the snatters were trippin' him."

The romance had gone out of the day for her, but she persevered with her walk as one who would not admit defeat and took herself up the Quarry Lane. It was a scorching hot day and the baby grew fractious, but Teesie jiggled the pram a bit and pressed on. She noticed some beautiful wild flowers growing in the fields alongside the road, and she pulled the pram into the hedge while she went to gather some. She became intent on her task, indeed totally engrossed in it, and soon had a fine bouquet to bring home. She presented it in triumph to her mother and was praised for being a good and thoughtful girl, and probably given a 'piece' for herself, to assuage the hunger that seems permanently to afflict children of a certain age, normally between two and twenty-three. A 'piece', for anyone under the age of fifty who might be tempted to think the term merely referred to a portion or segment, in a purely abstract sense, was the forerunner of the hamburger as the preferred snack of the under tens. It consisted of a doorstep of batch loaf liberally spread with butter and, on good days, strawberry jam. I never ate one in my life, being, to my mother's continual despair, a finicky eater, but all my pals, having normal healthy appetites, were reared on them.

When Teesie, après piece, had been in the house for some three-quarters of an hour, a thought struck her. Hadn't she forgotten something? Surely she had left the house that morning with something that she didn't remember bringing home? Enlightenment dawned with a painful shock. She had completely forgotten baby Joe in his pram, in the hedge, halfway up the Quarry Lane. Wordlessly she fled back as fast as her legs would carry her, her heart in her mouth, terrified of what she might – or might not – find, but discovered him quite safe, though if possible even more unattractive, due to the ravages of a warm day, the want of sustenance, and the bad temper this combination had produced.

"The only thing that kept me from panicking altogether," she told us, "was that he was so ugly I was fairly sure no one would want to kidnap him."

They say the whirligig of time brings in its revenges. One night many years later Teesie was about to be delivered of a child of her own, and being unable to sleep went looking for something to take her mind off her condition. "Billy," she said to her husband, "let me put your hair in curlers, it'll pass the time."

Billy, a fine man with a most easy-going demeanour as well as a head of thick dark hair, agreed. In later years when I knew him, he had begun to go grey, and the salt-and-pepper effect thus produced earned him the nickname of 'The Badger.' But tonight Teesie curled and crimped until a particularly sharp contraction told her that the baby was not about to wait much longer and she told Billy he had better fetch the doctor and pronto. He dashed off at once, hared out to Thomas Street, and raised whichever doctor was on call, quite possibly Dr. Campbell or Dr. Burley, who bade the expectant father wait and drive back with him in his car. When they got to the Donaghmore Road and Billy indicated that they had arrived at their destination, the doctor regarded him for a moment consideringly.

"Are you sure?" he enquired. Billy stared.

"Of course I'm sure," he spluttered. "Do you not think I know where I live?"

"It's not that," the doctor smiled. "I just wondered if you wanted me to drive you on up the road to Omagh."[5]

Only then did Billy realise he still had his hair in curlers.

[5] The location of 'The Big House', or lunatic asylum, long gone because of care in the community and political correctness, but back then, a place to which you were often metaphorically consigned if you did or said something daft.

Poker

Aideen and a Round Table

'Poker' (not her real name, as they say in all the best news reports), had so many idiosyncrasies that if she didn't exist, my mother would have had to invent her. Maureen Campbell was a mistress of impersonation, and Poker was one of her favourite subjects, not least because of her annoying habit of reinforcing everything she said with painful digs to your ribs. We always positioned her well away from other human beings in deference to their safety, but she manoeuvred round until she had someone – usually my mother – within range. She had a breathy way of speaking and a tendency to say, "Uh-huh, uh-huh" in response to any conversation addressed to her, that was also grist to my mother's mill.

She was not known for her generosity – she would skin a flea for its hide – and my mother asserted that when she made tomato sandwiches, a great standby in those days and not just for funerals, she only used the seeds. My grandmother used to visit Poker and her Mamma, and there was always a row between my mother and Mona as to who should accompany her, both of them determined that the honour should fall to the other one. Whoever drew the short straw was well warned by Granny Campbell that even though they would be offered supper, their hostess's earnest hope would be that they wouldn't eat very much, so they always fortified themselves well before they left their own house. On one occasion, Granny having a migraine, Mona and Maureen were going together, with me as the third member of the foraging party, but I, as a picky eater, posed no threat.

They reckoned without the Round Table.

Supper was served in the grand style at a large rosewood table of circular design, supported by one huge ornately carved central leg. At four years old I had never seen anything like it, and was totally fascinated. Accordingly, anything that was on it must perforce be of equal fascination and I fell to with a will, my mother and my aunt consequently eating less, remembering that Poker expected some food to be left on the table at the end of the repast, and there was little enough to begin with. Then I observed,

"That's a lovely wee butter dish." Everyone smiled. So far so good. "It's a pity they don't have more butter on it."

Several awkward minutes later I asked my aunt,

"Do you think I could have some more bread and jam?"

Poker gritted her teeth and dived into the kitchen, whence she emerged with half a slice of bread on a plate. "Here's the jam," she stammered, fumbling the dish in my general direction.

"Thank you," I said, before turning to my aunt. "But will you please put it on for me, Posy, because Poker doesn't put enough?"

My mother said it was the only time in her life that she regretted my being such a clear speaker.

Poker visited with us regularly for as long as I can remember, but disliked having to return the favour (no doubt in case they brought me), but she always felt inclined to issue an invitation, to preserve the niceties of social intercourse. This she hedged about with so many provisos that it became well-nigh impossible to accept, even if we had wanted to.

"You'll come down and see me, after the winter nights."

"Come down now, when the nights are a wee bit longer."

"Come some night when the mission's over."

"Call in when the school holidays start… when the schools are back… when your visitors go…"

But one day during my student days in the mid-1970s, she met us in The Square.

"You must come down and see me," she enthused, "after the Troubles."

I wonder if she has spoken to General Sir John de Chastelain lately?

We were not the only ones Poker's family didn't want. This was an honour we shared with most breathing creatures. Gerald Sheeran, who used to go from house to house with football pools[6] had occasion to call on them, and he told us that though he knocked and banged and tirled at the pin, there was no answer. Knowing their almost pathological hatred of callers, and being himself of a peculiar turn of mind, he determined to lay siege, and settled himself in for a long haul. After a few unresponsive minutes, he approached the curtained window off to one side of the door and, shading his eyes with his hand, attempted to peer through the glass. Two pairs of eyes looked solemnly back at him. Satisfied that his quarry was at home, and alive, he resumed the knocking. After a further five minutes, Poker and her mother came to the door, dressed for travel.

"Oh, Gerald!" trilled Mamma. "Oh dear, ha ha, we're just going out. We're catching the six o'clock bus to Stewartstown."

Gerald made a great show of consulting his watch, regarding it with close attention for a few seconds.

---

[6] The YP Pools were printed on pink or yellow sheets, and Gerald used one to wrap up the two biscuits he sometimes brought to Maureen's house to have with his tea. The package would be tied neatly with fine string, which he retained for future use.

———— ∞ ————

"In that case," he informed them, "you are destined to be disappointed. The time now is approaching six forty-seven, so I'm afraid you have missed it."

Poker had an insatiable appetite for news, though to be fair she was not a gossip and never repeated anything she heard, but her need to acquire gobbets of information bordered upon an addiction. We hadn't been long moved in to Ballysaggart when she came to see us. She positioned herself on the couch in front of the window, kneeling so that she could look out at the other houses in the square, and under cover of admiring the garden, tried to elicit as much information as she could about our new neighbours. The conversation – I use the term loosely – went something like this.

"Them's lovely wee flowers, Maureen. Who lives in that house over there?"

"Your mother was great with the roses too. Who's that going into that wee bungalow?"

"It's great to live out in the country." (We didn't). "Would that be so-and-so I see going in there?"

This inquisition got short shrift from my mother, for three reasons: she detested nosiness; she genuinely didn't know any of the neighbours at that stage; and worst of all, in order to carry out her surveillance, Poker had trailed the curtain halfway off the window with a none too gentle hand, and if there was one thing my mother was fussy about, it was the draping of her curtains. She even had my dad bring her a long wooden pole from work so that she could arrange the pleats evenly. She was quite tiny, a mere handful, who, she insisted, was growing down to the ground like a cow's tail as she got older, and therefore couldn't reach the top, yet the best efforts of Swish rails and Rufflette tape did not satisfy her eagle eye.

Jimmy McNally used to visit our house before my mum was married, in the days when she was working in Coagh, and for some reason his visits tended to coincide with Poker's. He loved a good night's crack, and her constant fishing for banalities finally

———— ∞ ————

drove him to desperate measures. He decided to inform Poker that he had gone deaf, and the Campbells were instructed to play along. Granny said he might do as he pleased as long as he didn't refer to her, for while she kept her head down over her embroidery she could manage to keep a straight face, but Jimmy had other ideas.

No one took his threat seriously, but Jimmy was a man of his word. The next night, as soon as she arrived, he lapsed into a morose silence, and only grunted when she addressed him. Finally in response to a nod and a wink, my mother broke the news that Jimmy had gone deaf due to an infection, and there followed a few weeks of sublime farce. Poker insisted on addressing remarks to Jimmy in stentorian tones, he persisted in misunderstanding her, and fabricated the persona of a man who genuinely can't hear but stubbornly pretends that he can.

Poker: Wasn't it sad, that woman dying on the train to Belfast?

Jimmy: Drowned in a drain? God help us.

Poker: Pull up to the range, Jimmy.

Jimmy: Get rid of them, Mrs. Campbell, get rid of them. Dogs with the mange will nivver be any good.

Jimmy: What happened that wee woman that died there from Irish Street?

Granny: I think it was cancer.

Jimmy: What?

Poker: Cancer! A tumour!

Jimmy: Be Jaysus it's no rumour if Mrs. Campbell has it.

The girls took huge delight in trying to second-guess where the conversation might lead, but Jimmy was always one step ahead. One night the kettle, a whistler, was put on for supper. Just as it reached its shrill, ear-shattering, crescendo, Jimmy cocked his head quizzically.

"Mrs. Campbell, pardon me for asking, and no offence to a decent woman like yourself, but would you have mice? It's just that I can hear a faint squeaking in the distance…"

Every night after that, Poker would exhort my mum in ringing

———— ∞ ————

tones, "Put on the whistling kettle!" and chortle like an over-grown schoolgirl as Jimmy kept up the suspicion of mice, with many apologies to my grandmother. She also took it upon herself to impart to Jimmy anything she thought might be of interest to him. She had never learned the trick of speaking to the hard of hearing by sitting directly in front of them and speaking slowly and clearly. Instead her tactics involved sitting beside him, grab-bing him by the lapel, dragging his ear to within an inch of her mouth, and shrieking at him.

"And him that can hear the flies coughing," my mother observed ruefully.

One evening, just before Poker's arrival, Jimmy remarked to my grandmother, "What am I like, Mrs. Campbell: making an eejit of myself to make another eejit laugh!"

"It's your own fault, Jimmy," Granny told him. "I've no sym-pathy for you."

"Och, now, Mrs. Campbell, sure I was desperate."

Poker was always anxious for news of Jimmy's family, so one night he told her his wife was dying, and that he would be left with eleven children, whom he then proceeded to name: Moses-Ezekiel, Ponsomby-Stepens, Zachariah-Iscariot, and a string of other names that would never have been used in the nomencla-ture of Dungannon in the 1940s, or indeed for long afterwards. The wife's progress was documented in a series of misunderstand-ings and double entendres for the next few weeks, until he told them things had reached crisis point, and he was now looking about for a replacement. Poker was horrified, and told the fam-ily so in a series of angry asides that of course were fully audible to Jimmy. He favoured her with a slanting glance and told my grandmother,

"I've me eye on somebody already. You need to be quick off the mark these days, good women are scarce. I know a man out the Donaghmore Road, and his two wives baked out of the same bag of flour." He glanced at Poker's legs which were not, to put it kindly, the type that you would use to advertise hosiery. My mother's other name for her was Longtrams. "Did you know him, Mrs. Campbell? He owned that pub, The Besom Shafts."

He ogled Poker and spat on his hands before rubbing them together with a sly grin.

"No matter. I've another in me blinker, and by God she is a clinker!"

She didn't come back for weeks, until she met Jimmy in town and elicited the intelligence that though 'they were turning her on sheets', the wife was recovering well, but for all that, her visits and his somehow ceased to coincide.

Years later we met Jimmy and he told us,

"Be God, wait'll you hear. I had a narrow escape the other day. I went into that wee shop where Poker works and there she was behind the counter. Just in time I remembered I was supposed to be deaf and I roared at her, 'GIVVUS A STAMP!'"

It takes a liar to have a good memory.

Mum and her pal Gogga Rice had, for reasons best known to two teenagers who enjoyed a laugh, arranged to go for a walk with Poker's sister, Gladys, promising to call for her. The door was opened by Gladys's mother, whose tendency to dress in frills and flounces that were much too young for her was, according to my mum who had a word for everything, *flandrican*. The effect was not diminished by her giddy manner.

"Oh dear, ha ha, oh my, Gladys had to go out, she's terribly sorry, hee hee, call again."

Veronica, like Gerald, was not so easily put off, and managed to get inside the house, trailing my mum in her wake.

"We'll wait for her," offered Gogga.

"Oh no, ha ha, she might be ages, oh dear me…"

At this point my mum noticed Gogga winking conspiratorially at her and gesturing madly with her head, rolling her eyes. Picking up the clue, Maureen meandered over to where a large sofa occupied the centre of the room. There on the other side of it crouched Gladys, out of sight but not, as it happened, out

———— ∞ ————

of mind. My mother burst out laughing, but Gladys rose to the occasion.

"Glory be to God, I'm painting my chilblains," she informed them. With iodine, for those of you too young to know. There was, as Jane Eyre once memorably observed, no possibility of taking a walk that evening.

Gladys and Poker had a brother of whom I remember very little save for his manner of choosing his reading matter, which, in all my years as a librarian, I have found to be quite unique. Like all great discoveries, it was made by accident, by my Uncle Wilf, who was doing a wee job for Joe Campbell (yes, another of those Campbells, no relation, just another branch of the great Tyrone clan, who, my mother insisted, went from here to Scotland and colonized it, and definitely not the other way about!). Joe had a wee shop in William Street, one of many in Dungannon of which it might have been said that when the press door was open, the shop was shut, but despite the limitations of space it sold a wide variety of goods, and along one wall there were several shelves full of paperbacks.

Wilf was down on his hunkers behind the counter working, Joe having nipped into the kitchen behind the shop for a cup of tea, leaving instructions that if a customer presented himself, Wilf was to call him. Wilf looked up to see Poker's brother, Mick, who explained that he was here to choose a few books and would call Joe himself when he was ready. Wilf resumed his work, and after a minute heard a most peculiar chant:

"I t'ought I taw a puddy tat a-creeping up on me."

He paused, frowned, shifted the Woodbine to the other side of his mouth, listened. It came again. Slowly he laid down his tools and peered above the counter. There was Mick, counting across the spines of the books with the index and middle fingers of his right hand, slowly repeating the rhyme. Wherever his finger happened to alight as the chant ended, this was the book selected for examination. He had obviously taken to heart the advice that you should never judge a book by its cover.

The King of North Carolina

Passage Fishermen

"Anybody wanting to use the bathroom, go now," my dad would say, "for I'm going to haul her up on the beach."

He was off for his Friday night bath, the one he could soak in and take his time over, and sometimes an alternative call might float down the stairs: "I'm away to scrape the bottom."

This had nothing to do with human anatomy, but instead referred to the custom of taking a boat out of the water at the end of the season and scraping all the accumulated sand, grit, and especially barnacles, off the hull, before cleaning her down to make ready for the next outing. Growing up in a fishing village where the people who didn't make their living from the sea were few and far between, it's no wonder my father's conversation was peppered with imagery from the maritime world, his vocabulary richly coloured by it. Boats also gave him one of his favourite phrases to describe someone of ample girth: "That one's broad about the beam." And where a Dungannon man might have

——————— ✑ ———————

said, "I'm all right, Jack," my dad always said, "Haul up the ladder, Jack, I'm safely aboard."

He told me once of a friend of his who, coming home from Mass one Sunday, was horrified to come upon a lady taken short by the call of nature, who had retreated into the hedgerow to do what she had to do. John made himself as scarce as he could, mortified, but as he told my dad later,

"It was me that was embarrassed, Pat, not yer woman. She just up canvas and down linen[7] without batting an eye, and waved at me as I passed!"

Gogga Rice had a similar experience, only this time it was she who was caught out in need of facilities. She was coming round the Quarry Lane in Dungannon which in those days was the middle of nowhere with not a house on it, and she was desperate. She looked around, scanned the horizon, but there was no one in sight. As she rose from the ditch and made to resume her walk she heard a piercing wolf whistle.

"Jaysus, Campbell" – she always used my mother's surname – "What do you think it was? Two telegraph engineers on top of a pole right above my head!"

The Passage men knew a thing or two about weather forecasting. They had to; their livelihoods depended upon it. My dad would look out of an evening when the wind blew up a squall and say, "Southerly wind and rain for the Passage taypots," for on that part of the coast a southerly breeze meant a good catch of fish, and thus plenty to eat. Of course, they weren't the only ones to welcome a south wind, for as the old rhyme tells us,

When the wind is in the East, 'tis neither good for man nor beast.
When the wind is in the North, the skilful fisher goes not forth.
When the wind is in the South, it blows the bait in the fish's mouth.
When the wind is in the West, then it is at its very best.

[7] Like a ship in full sail

———————

There was a spot in Passage down by the breakwater known as the Men's Walk, and here the menfolk would gather to chew the fat, discuss the day's headlines and generally put the world to rights. At one time every town or village had such a meeting place. In Dungannon it was the Electric Corner, so called, not because of the calibre of the men who congregated there, but because the old Electricity Board showrooms occupied that spot where Scotch Street and Irish Street meet. Later on when the council found sufficient funds to put a bench at the foot of The Square, the men moved over there.

One of the stalwarts of the Men's Walk was Mickey Hennessey, and his was the definitive opinion on the morrow's weather. Not that he made up his mind in a hurry. He would patrol from one end of the Walk to the other four or five times, admittedly not a great distance, glance down the estuary towards the open sea, spit once or twice and say, "My Jesus, what is it going to be or what?" Then he would give his decision. If a big wind was anticipated he would advise, "It's going to blow a criminjer!" A light wind, especially one of those little breezes that blows up from nowhere, was a *she-ghee,* from the Irish *sí gaoth* or fairy wind. If there was frost in the air he would warn, "A snipe'll not walk it in the morning." But if Mickey wasn't about you could try a spot of DIY forecasting by reading the signs, such as *Mackerel skies and mares' tails make big ships wear small sails,* for this cloud formation warned of approaching storms. And if you'd ever seen the wind chasing white wisps of cloud along the Suir inlet on a blustery day, you'd know that they look exactly like the tail of some demonic mare in flight across the heavens!

My acquaintance with Passage began when we went down for the funeral of my dear Aunt Lil Sheeran, really my great-aunt, who had been a teacher in London, living in a house in Bromley called 'Sunny Corner' – straight out of Enid Blyton! When she developed breast cancer, she came home to die. Lil and I never met but conducted a lifelong correspondence by letter, and I knew her as well as it is possible to know anyone, and I think she knew me just the same! Tragically she and my Uncle Charlie were undergoing treatment for cancer at the same time, and throughout her long illness she characteristically made light of her own suffering and bent all her concern on him. In one of her last letters to us in October 1966 she wrote,

> *Here I am in the old Home. I arrived last Sat. after a very calm journey. I travelled 1st class all the way from Paddington to Waterford... so it was quite comfortable... Mine was a big op but I am going on fine now, no dressings, the whole thing is all cleared up wonderful. I want you to know that in all my fright & pain I never forgot to pray for Charlie & I do hope he is getting on alright.*

At the time, although I was aware that Lil was sick, I had no idea of how much she suffered for the details were kept from me, and it is only in reading the letters now that I begin to see how things were. She could no longer work and went to stay with a friend, for she had not married, partly, I guess, because her father was one of the old style Edwardian patriarchs who thought that nobody was good enough for his girls, with the result that each suitor was summarily dismissed and often the four sisters – Margaret, known as Cis, who eventually became my grandmother D'Arcy, Lil, Mai, and the baby, Rosie – were forced to conduct their romances in secret. It's a miracle he approved of Mr. D'Arcy, but maybe he was going through a literary phase. The girls grew tired of this tyranny and Lil and Mai fled to London. Rose remained at home, but only Margaret married.

Lil's friend had her own problems for her husband was, in Lil's view, 'heading for a nervous breakdown', and though we know little more than that, we know that he was not kindly disposed towards Lil, and she moved on to stay with another friend. She was busy putting her affairs in order and waiting for a sum of money to be released from a bequest that had been made to her, so things were very unsatisfactory. She refers only to having 'a very trying time', but her faith shines through it all like a beacon and she constantly tells us that prayer got her through some very dark places. Oddly enough, this conviction that God would sort things out was something she shared with Charlie, the deep-seated belief in a supreme and benevolent Power sustaining them both to the end. But if, as we now believe, cancer is exacerbated by stress, it's no wonder that when she finally made it home it was only to be a few months before she passed away. And Charlie didn't make it past Christmas, for he died on December 8th 1966.

Lil always remembered birthdays and special occasions, and a few weeks before mine, I would get a letter containing the magic words, *What would you like for your birthday?* The only one she ever missed was when she was in hospital for her cancer operation, and even then we find her writing shortly after,

> *I am sure Aideen wondered she never got the birthday gift from me but I never thought I would be in Hosp. I will send her some cash soon, very soon, to get slippers.*

I wasn't allowed to be greedy, so I had to choose carefully and ask for only one thing, but when the parcel came, it was like Mary Poppins's carpet bag. There in the middle would be the requested gift, always cutting edge since it came from London and in those days you really couldn't buy the like in Dungannon, surrounded by an array of smaller items, all unusual, all beautiful and very carefully chosen, like the Easter egg where the two halves formed a baby's cradle, complete with twin occupants, frilly pillows and coverlet, all crafted from fondant icing. And no matter what she sent in the way of clothes, it always seemed to fit. I have never known anyone else who had this happy knack of selecting wonderful gifts, and presenting them in such a novel manner. She was a lovely, lovely woman, and if I have any regrets about her now it is simply that I didn't know quite how special she was when she was alive. I was far too young to understand and I can only say that I loved her dearly, and always lived with the dream of meeting up with her one day. I still hope to do that.

The night before we were due to travel down for the funeral I opened the door to a tall RUC officer who had come to tell my dad that his aunt had died in County Waterford, a job the police often had to do in the days before there was a phone in every house. My dad was taken aback. He knew she was dead, we were going down on the morrow… However, this was not Auntie Lil, but Aunt Mai, whose life had been snuffed out by a massive heart attack only days after her sister's death, as she stood in the kitchen washing dishes, so we buried two family members that week, leaving behind only two of the four sisters, and Uncle Eugene, always called Sonny. He was the only brother, and he had made his home in Liverpool, where he married and fathered one son, Tom, who acted as best man at my parents' wedding. Eugene was stocky and dapper with a shock of snow-white hair that grew back from his forehead in waves, exactly like my dad's. They also shared a slight tendency to deafness. He was great crack, and was the best card-trickster I ever came across. He always saved a slab of his after-dinner ice-cream for me, so I probably left Passage with my puppy-fat converted into full-grown hound fat, but did I care? Not one jot.

The journey to Passage was a mammoth undertaking, and lasted all day. We got a taxi to The Square where we caught a bus to Portadown, there to embark by train for Dublin. Arrived in Connolly Station we had a wait of several hours so we would go in search of lunch, once we had stowed our cases in the left luggage lockers, and if we were very fortunate there might be a rattle round a bookshop. Then we got a taxi to Heuston Station whence the trains for the south departed, and eventually we'd arrive in Waterford, mid-way through a summer's evening. It was a further seven miles to Passage, so we had to get another taxi, and I can still remember the lift of the heart, the intake of breath, as the car swept round the bend of the road and the Suir estuary opened up in front of us, the water glittering like the path to the enchanted isles below, with the villages of Ballyhack, Duncannon, and Arthurstown on the opposite shore, and on our side of the river, Passage, with its decent houses, its two or three shops, and its two pubs.

One of these was run by Lily White and her husband Dick, who, on being introduced to my mother, shook her hand and greeted her with "Ireland awoke…"

"Dungannon spoke," she replied, never to be outdone when it came to poetry, and made a friend for life. His favourite book was *Knocknagow* by Charles J Kickham, and when he got a few too many he would become lachrymose and introverted, and murmur tearfully "Kickham, boy; Kickham," in response to questions as to what ailed him.

I had a brush with Kickham once, though it was a while before I knew it. Some evenings I would have occasion to go over to Kathleen's shop on the Donaghmore Road. My mother was debarred from going, because Daddy knew if she went, she'd be there for an hour or more, yarning, whereas if I went I'd come back in reasonable time with whatever message I had been sent for. Unless I met Paddy.

Paddy was a respectable farmer from 'out the road', which might have meant anything from the Sprickley Well to Carrickmore. He was low-set, neat of himself, and always wore a flat dun-coloured cap and dealin' boots, and he took a wee drink in Daly's. On the way home he would wander in for a chat with Kathleen, and anyone else who might listen. The first night I met him I was wearing my hair loose down my back, and it was long enough at this stage of my life for me to sit on. It fell, like the piano in Service's *Malamute Saloon,* in the way of his wandering gaze. He lurched towards me, peered blearily into my surprised face, and instructed Kathleen to "give that wee girl a bar of chocolate", then he gently stroked my hair, and murmured,

She lived beside the Anner,
At the foot of Slieve-na-mon,
A gentle Irish Colleen
With mild eyes like the dawn.

There followed a deal more that I couldn't make head nor tail of, but though I seized the opportunity provided by the entrance of another customer to flee, I was not frightened, for there was nothing intimidatory about him. I was, if anything, slightly embarrassed. Of course I got told off for being away as long as my mother.

"A joult in the mare is a joult in the foal," and my long-suffering father shook his head.

Over the next few weeks my path and Paddy's crossed regularly. I always got my bar of chocolate, he always stroked my hair and quoted these lines. I had told my mum what kept me on these occasions, and she took it in her stride. I think she knew my serenader, as in knowing his provenance and background, and she also understood how easy it is to get caught up in a conversation that you can't get out of.

"What do you be talking about?" Mona asked me in deep amusement one night.

"You couldn't call it talking, exactly," I told her. "It's always the same rigmarole of a poem, and I can't for the life of me figure out why I should get the honour."

"How does it go?" She was like a sniffer dog on speed when a poem was mentioned.

"Something about living beside the Anner, wherever that is."

The two sisters were smiling knowingly, nodding their heads. I rolled my eyes.

"Go on then, enlighten me."

"It's by Charles Kickham –"

"– who wrote *Knocknagow* –"

"It's your hair…"

"But why?"

———— ∞ ————

I can see them now, mum crossing an elegant leg, Mona leaning forward with her hands clasped around one of her knees, quoting practically line about as they each lit up a Kensitas tipped:

> *Her lips were dewy rosebuds,*
> *Her teeth were pearls rare,*
> *And a snow-drift 'neath a beechen bough*
> *Her neck and nut-brown hair.*

"Real sentimental stuff, kind of like *From a Munster vale they brought her...*"[8]

"I suppose she dies?"

"Oh aye, she goes out to America to work and send money home, and of course she's worked to death, but manages to write a last letter:

> *'Write word to my dear mother,*
> *Say we'll meet with God above,*
> *And tell my little brothers*
> *I send them all my love.*
> *May the angels ever guard them*
> *Is their dying sister's prayer' —*
> *And folded in the letter*
> *Was a braid of nut-brown hair.'"*

"So you see, the hair is, as Jeeves might have said to Bertie, of the essence." We were reading P G Wodehouse at the time.

"Imagine he knows poetry by Kickham!"

"Why wouldn't he?" Mum enquired.

I couldn't think of any good reason when I put my mind to it, so I changed tack.

"God help him, I suppose he loves that stuff."

Posy looked at me.

[8] *The Dying Girl* by Richard D'Alton Williams

———————

"It might seem sentimental to us," she pointed out, "but an awful lot of people did have to leave home like that years ago, and hundreds of them died out in America without ever seeing home or family again."

Chastened, I hoked out the poem in one of our old issues of Walton's *Irish Fireside Songs*.

"You didn't tell me she was a stunner," I complained, quoting:

> *The widow's brown-haired daughter*
> *Was the loveliest of the throng.*

Daddy was passing by on his way up to Charlie's.
"Black cat, black kitten," he muttered.

My dad was having a quiet one in Lily's one night with his friend John Baston, who ordered a wee whiskey.

"Have you any ice?" he asked the barmaid.

"We're out of ice," she replied tartly.

"You could give it a coul' look then," suggested John.

It might have been the same evening that they struck up a conversation with an old-timer who had spent most of his life at sea.

"Things are not the same now," he complained. "I remember a time in my young day when we had wooden ships and iron men. Now we have iron ships and wooden men, and we're no better aff for it."

He told them that what he missed most when he was at sea was his drink, a ball and a bottle, or to you and me, a wee whiskey and a bottle of Guinness – no fancy draught then!

"I do be looking forward to that drink for days when we're on the way home," he said, wiping the froth off his mouth with a satisfied smack of the lips. "And when I get a couple of bottles down me, I can fart like a stone horse!"

Man might not live on bread alone, but yeast in some forms is a great comforter!

Not all creatures thrive on alcohol; witness Johnny 'Leather's' three cats. In the days before milk came neatly packaged and pasteurised in doorstep bottles, you could buy it out of those big churns that now, sterilised and painted, form the centrepiece of many a fancy gift-shop. You only had to provide your own container. Leather went to the shop every day with his jug, the three cats walking in stately procession behind him. On the home stretch, he would turn around every few strides and pour a drop of milk onto the street as a treat for the cats to lap. One day he set off on quite another errand, armed with his container – we can only hope it wasn't the same jug, but the cats were taking no chances, and they accompanied him as usual. On the way home there was no turning, no outpouring of largesse, and the felines were put out as only felines know how to be. They set up a wailing and a mewling to show what they thought of this kind of treatment, so Leather turned around and held the jug down at nose level (cat's, that is) for them to take a good sniff.

"Paraffin oil, if yiz wants to know," he informed them.

Sometimes a pub would host a traditional music session, with everybody putting in their three ha'pence worth – fiddles, bodhráns, flutes, tin whistles, concertinas, all playing tunes with those wonderfully evocative titles: *The Maid Behind the Barrel, The Hen's March Over the Midden, The Stack of Barley*. Daddy was at a session in Clare one night, and he noticed that one of the musicians had returned from a visit to the smallest room without doing up his trousers. The man was so engrossed in his fiddling that he hadn't noticed, so after a minute or two, Daddy leant over and whispered,

"Jimmy! Your fly's open."

Jimmy fiddled on without a pause, hissing out of the side of his mouth,

"Whistle a few bars for me now, and if I recognise it I'll play it for you."

——— ∽ ———

As a child I naturally assumed that my parents knew everything, but if ever I asked Daddy the name of an Irish tune, he always gave the same answer: "That's *The Top of the Cork Road.*" And I always believed him. Now I know that it hardly mattered, for to the untutored ear it is hard to distinguish one tune from another, but when the slide from piece to piece is so seamless, and the combination so adrenaline-boosting, no one really cares. In any case, they say if you know the names of all the tunes, you don't know enough of them, but Daddy was far more knowledgeable about light classical music and operetta, which was his real love, and could often be heard singing something from *Maritana,* which was written by another Waterford man, William Wallace, or *The Lily of Killarney.* Consequently, what I know about seventies' pop music I learned retrospectively, for I was brought up on *The Student Prince* and *Lilac Time.* If pressed, or if he had had a couple of wee ones, Daddy would sing his party piece, *The Miller's Daughter,* and though he had no voice, he could carry a tune. One of his favourite works was Gounod's *Faust,* and I remember my delight when I found a boxed set of the complete opera on three vinyl discs in a wee shop in Dublin called 'Opus', and gave it to him one Christmas. I learned the words to *The Soldiers' Chorus,* and could sing along with him:

> *Glory and love to the men of old!*
> *Their sons may copy their virtues bold!*
> *Courage in heart and a sword in hand,*
> *Ready to fight, ready to die, for fatherland!*

He reminisced with real fondness about the pantomimes they staged when he was young, with stalwarts like Dick Galvin, or his pal John Baldwin, and once with the assistance of Belgian musical director M. Georges Minnes, who later taught me in St. Patrick's Girls' Academy in Dungannon before becoming organist at St. Patrick's Cathedral in Armagh. His favourites were *Dick*

Whittington and *Rumpelstiltskin,* and he could sing a verse or two from each of them:

> *Turn again Dick Whittington,*
> *Thrice Lord Mayor of London Town…*

> *Rumpelstiltskin, Rumpelstiltskin,*
> *Oh, he could sew, he could sew,*
> *That tailor man could sew!*
> *He could sew a seam in a pale moonbeam*
> *Or mend a dress,*
> *Or repair a tear in your happiness,*
> *Oh ho! That tailor man could sew!*

But when all the jollification was over and the greasepaint had worn off, there was no better way to pass an evening than with a quiet pint in Lily's or Twomey's. In the days – well before my time – when there were eight pubs in Passage it was easy to get one too many, for the pub was where all the news was to be had, information about the fishing, news of births and deaths, and some felt it necessary to visit all the watering holes in case they missed something. There was one such imbiber who, after eight stops and at least as many pints, was making his way home up by Crooke graveyard. He had to take a shortcut through the little Protestant cemetery, and then the slightly larger Catholic cemetery, in order to get home, but being a bit unsteady, he fell over his feet and cowped into a freshly dug grave that had been made ready for an interment the following day. He slept soundly and was awakened next morning by a glorious sunrise coming up over Duncannon. He looked towards it.

"Glory be to God!" he cried. "The last day, and I'm the first up!"

There was a wealthy but eccentric brother and sister living near Passage many years ago, and when the brother died he was buried in the family vault. For two nights the sister visited the place to light candles and say prayers, and she prefaced the recital by intoning three times, "Joshua, are your feet cold?"

On the third night, a gentleman of the roads had wandered in to take shelter behind one of the tombstones, as was not uncommon, and he had a naggin of whiskey with him, which he swigged till he fell asleep. He woke to hear the cry of, "Joshua, are your feet cold?" and looked about him. Not knowing that the lady had been recently bereaved and that this was the opening chorus of a ritual that clearly gave her comfort, his whiskey-soaked brain understood that it was his welfare she was concerned with, and as she enquired for the third time, "Joshua, are your feet cold?" he rose from behind the stone with a grin, scratched himself, and answered,

"No, my lady, but me arse is none too warm."

It was in Lily's pub that my dad picked up the phrase he later habitually employed when he got tired of waiting for something.

There were two oul' fellas who used to frequent the bar during daylight hours. They paid for their rounds alternately, and their custom was to make each drink last as long as possible while they enjoyed whatever company might wander in off the street. One day, one of them had finished his pint before the other and there was no sign of a replacement being ordered up. After a few nods and winks which were stolidly ignored, our man turned to the barmaid and said,

"What did the king of North Carolina say to the king of South Carolina?"

"God, I don't know, Dan," she said. "What did he say?"

Dan glowered at his companion and replied in an exaggerated drawl,

"It's a long time between drinks."

The Post Office was run by Kitten Donnelly, whose given name was probably Kathleen. She kept a pencil tied to the outside of

the mesh that separated her from her customers, one of those indelible ones that writes normally when dry but when wetted writes in a lurid shade of purple. I remember we had one in our house but I only got to use it by stealth, for they were widely considered to be poisonous. I don't actually know what they were for, but we used ours to address packages, and I have a notion that they might have been used for telegrams. Kitten was serving one of the village's fine ladies, when she observed her popping the pencil into her mouth and sucking it to produce the violet – or violent – effect.. She was about to repeat the procedure when Kitten advised,

"I don't think you should do that, they say they're poison."

Whether it was simply that the lady did not like to be admonished, or whether she had just swallowed the antidote I know not, but she withered Kitten with a scowl and shot back,

"Fancy, fancy! I love the taste of poison!" before shoving the pencil back in her mouth. She would have got her answer in Dungannon, from the elderly man who was advising a young colleague not to do something because it was dangerous. When the youth persisted in his folly the oul' fellow turned aside with a contemptuous spit. "Whatever the hell you like," he remarked, and left him to it. Like Willy's donkey.

Willy travelled everywhere in a donkey and cart, and one night the local wags decided to play a trick on him. He arrived for his ceilidh at one of his regular calling houses and as was his custom, left the donkey harnessed in the shafts with a bit of feed, to stand there and wait for his return. The lads crept up and unhooked the animal from the traces, opened a nearby field gate and led it inside, then wheeled the cart over, poked the shafts through the bars and harnessed the ass up again. When Willy came out a couple of hours later and maybe with a drop of potín to keep out the cold, he was annoyed to find the ass no longer where he had left it, but he spotted it soon enough and dandered over to the gateway. He stood for a moment assessing the situation, the ass on one side of the gate, the cart on the other, but the harnessing all intact. He leant over and looked the donkey straight in the face.

"You got yourself into it, and you can get yourself out of it," he told it. And walked home.

Another of Kitten's customers was Moll Rook, whose real name was Mary Hearne. Molly was a common enough diminutive of Mary but I don't know why the family got the nickname *rook*. In Ballymulderg *rook* had unpleasant connotations, usually denoting someone who would defraud or cheat you. I remember Lizzie Larkin telling my grandmother that she intended to make a will, because "The dirty rooks of the M— family will never get my money." But I have no idea whether the word had the same meaning in County Waterford, nor do I think it would have been applied in this sense to Moll and her brothers. Moll arrived in the Post Office to send a telegram to her sister in England to advise her that her mother, who had been ailing for some time, was now very ill and was not expected to live much longer.

"How do you want me to phrase the message, Moll?" Kitten enquired.

"Och, Kitten girl, just put, *Ma drawing away mad Moll.*"

In middle life she put on a bit of weight around her tummy as many women do, and on days when she wasn't feeling her best, she would cradle her stomach in her clasped hands and give it a little rock saying, "Only for you I'd be a young girl the day!" She was a regular church-goer, a God-fearing woman, but she had an unusual way of asking the Lord into her heart. When she approached the altar to take Holy Communion she would stand for a moment, hands folded, eyes shut in silent prayer, then just before the priest proffered the Host, would strike her breast and enunciate in ringing tones,

"Jaysus jump into me stomach!"

She handled the money for the household, earned mainly from fishing, and used to keep the cash behind the Sacred Heart altar with its votive light that graced the walls of many an Irish house in days gone by. Come Friday, and one of the boys would ask,

———— ∞ ————

"Moll, where's the salmon money?" for they might have wanted to sink a pint or two as they caught up on the news of the village. And Moll would always give the same reply.

"Tis under the wee blue Jaysus."

But she had other phrases at her disposal which she demonstrated to great effect one day when things went against her.

One of the ways the fishermen could earn extra money was by acting as escorts to the big ships that went up the Suir towards Waterford. The river is tidal at Passage, and there are sand and mud-banks which could prove treacherous for the unwary, so when word came of a ship being expected, some of the men would go down and wait for her, and whoever 'got' her was sure of a bit of a bonus, always welcome. I suppose it was first come, first served, or that there was some sort of pecking order, but on this occasion there was word of a ship on the way from Gibraltar, and Moll's brothers, Geoff and Pat, were there to 'get' her, but she didn't arrive at the expected time. This was not unusual, so the brothers determined to wait, but like The Highwayman, she did not come in the morning, she did not come at noon. In fact, a whole week went by and still she had not come, but the brothers were tough men and were not prepared to let a small thing like a week's delay keep them from their bounty. They took it in turns to wait, but nine days later even they got discouraged and gave up the vigil. They were all gathered around the family table, Moll preparing dinner, when suddenly they heard the unmistakable sound of a ship's horn, the signal that a ship was coming up river and was in need of a pilot. The brothers, tired, dispirited, and disheartened, knew that they wouldn't make it down in time to get her, and that the privilege this time would fall to someone else. Moll went out to the gate and stared in disgust as she watched the ship breasting the waves towards the harbour. She shook her fist at it.

"Blow, you whore, blow!" she screeched at it, "after your nine days coming from the Rock!"

Lament for the Passage Fishermen

We were glad to see the herrings come
And the news was quickly spread,
We'd be free from harassing want this fall
And the wintry months ahead,
But 'twere better they'd stayed in distant parts
Where foam-lashed billows roll
For they brought us sorrow and aching hearts
And the sea has claimed its toll.

The world has known of Passage
Since the days of the Croppy Boy,
She is known again for her good men lost
Beneath an Autumn sky.
Brave Kirby, and Smiling Willie,
Young Rogers, and Quiet Joe,
Who went with the tide in the gloaming
And we did not see them go.

They are hardy folk, our fishermen,
And we owe them a deep, deep debt,
These harvesters of the troubled wave,
These men who heave the net.
Was there no one at hand to help them?
Well, this we can render yet,
The hapless ones they have left behind
Let us not forget.

Take them O Lord to Thy Sacred Heart,
Call them to walk with Thee,
Fisher...................
On Storm-tossed Galilee;
They've laboured and taken nothing
As they launched out into the deep
Till Thou camest to them on the waters
And called them home to sleep.

This lovely little lament for the victims of a drowning tragedy I found among Daddy's things long after he was able to tell me anything about it. I include it as a tribute to all the men who reap the harvest of the sea, for even today she is a hard mistress. I have no idea who wrote it, and unfortunately there are some words missing in Verse 4, but I still think it's worth preserving.

It wasn't only Passage men who lost their lives in the waters around Waterford. One of my dad's favourite reminiscences concerned the wreck of the *Alfred D Snow,* a cargo ship that sailed from San Francisco to Liverpool with a load of grain in the winter of 1887/88. Five months to sea she was hit by a fierce storm, and the captain had no alternative but to run for cover into Waterford harbour. The ship was blown off course and hit a sandbank at Broomhill Point, two miles south of Duncannon on the Wexford side of the Suir estuary. In response to her distress signals the crew of the Dunmore lifeboat was called out, but the coxswain, Captain Cherry, refused to launch her, saying that though the boat might live on such a stormy sea, the men could not. There was a pilot boat in Passage but it couldn't go out either, and though eventually the second coxswain, William Jones, agreed to captain the boat, with the help of a Welsh fisherman, Mr. G R Woods, it was too late. The ship was lost with all hands, and their memorial is a few graves on the south coast and a ballad, of disputed authorship, but probably from the pen of a Dunmore East woman, Nelty Woods. It was the fourth day of January, in 1888. My dad always maintained that if it hadn't been for the help of the Passage men the lifeboat could not have gone out, but I don't know if this is historical fact or parochial patriotism.

It was probably experiences such as this that prompted one of Daddy's most enduring – and endearing – habits. Every night on his way to bed, he would dip his fingers into the Holy Water font by the front door, sprinkle a drop on the ground and murmur, "For all travellers and sailors, and anyone out on the sea tonight…"

The Salmon of Knowledge

Patrick D'Arcy as a boy

As a boy, my dad would have killed for sausages, a predilection that lasted him all his life. In those days you didn't buy them in neat little packets wrapped in cling film, adulterated with additives and plumped up with water, but in a long string straight from the butcher's shop where they were made that very morning. One evening when he was only a grall of a lad, Daddy wandered into the kitchen where he espied a fine string of porkers, clearly intended for the evening's tea. His heart leapt up. Unfortunately so did the cat who had slipped in along with him. It made a grab for the sausages, seized them in its teeth, and shot out the door and down the street, with my father in hot pursuit. He chased it through the village, the cat zigzagging in and out of alleyways and gardens, the sausages trailing in the dirt, the young Pat always a stride or two behind. Finally, weary, tearful, and bereft, he made his way home, leaving the cat to enjoy its dinner. In later years we were holidaying in the village and met up with Mickey Hennessey.

———— ∞ ————

"Do you mind the day the cat stole the sausages, Pat?"

"I do indeed," laughed my dad.

"I often wondered," Mickey told him, "what exactly you were going to do with them if you had managed to get them back!"

His elder brother Tom was a fussy eater and liked everything just so before he could enjoy his food. My Grandmother D'Arcy and Aunt Rose, or Rosie, who had the best legs I've ever seen apart from my mother's, were both good cooks and always kept a dainty table, with laundered cloths, napkins, and, as was customary in those days, a bowl into which you could tip the dregs of your tea before you poured a second cup, so that you wouldn't be putting a beggar down on top of a gentleman. This was known as the slop bowl. It came as a great surprise when Tom started dining with the Hennessey family, a father and three sons, and no woman in the house so that things were, to put it mildly, a bit rough. Dinner usually consisted of some kind of fish, accompanied by a huge potful of potatoes which, when cooked, were tipped out onto the centre of the big wooden table for all to stretch or starve. You did get a plate for the fish. Tom always partook heartily of the fare and usually a glass of milk along with it. One evening he drank the cup of tea that followed and accepted the invitation for a refill.

"Where is the slop bowl?" enquired Tom, mindful of his manners. The brothers looked at him.

"Slash it on the flure, lad," they advised him.

They grew fine spuds in Passage. In Dungannon we always had mashed potatoes or champ, but in Passage I got my first taste of potatoes as they would have been eaten from time immemorial by our forefathers, big floury puffballs breaking out of their skins, crumbly and dry as a bone, crying out for a knob of butter, tasty as the first fruits of the Garden of Eden. They were served in a huge tureen that formed the centrepiece of the dinner table, with the fragrant steam getting your digestive juices off the starting blocks before you even sat down. Granny D'Arcy called them 'smilers', and it's a certainty that you'd be smiling as you ate them. In times gone by the potatoes would have been cooked in a pot oven or cauldron over the fire, then set beside the hearth to keep warm. Men coming in from the field would help themselves to a couple as they came in, maybe taking a pinch of salt from the wooden box by the wall, leaving plenty for the next wave of workers as they came home. A precursor of McDonald's as the fast food of the Irish.

In Passage too I first tasted salmon as in fish as opposed to salmon as in tin. My Aunt Mona and I were out walking when we were hailed by a friend, Tessie Gunnip, whose husband was a fisherman, and the best pilot on the south coast. She handed us a package wrapped in newspaper, cold, and surprisingly heavy.

"There now!" She was all smiles. "Take that down to Rosie."

We thanked her, and moved on.

"What is it?" I wanted to know. Mona wrinkled her nose and peered under a corner of the slightly damp paper.

"Some oul' fish."

"What'll we do with it?"

"I don't know. Should we throw it over that wall?"

"But it'll stink, and then somebody will find it and maybe tell Tessie." Passage in those days was very small.

We decided to bring it home to Rosie and chuck it in our own bin, but when we presented the fish and our plan to Aunt Rose she fell about laughing.

"God, girl, do you know what that is?" Two heads were shaken.

"It's a salmon. Have you any idea how much that's worth?"

We hadn't, and when she told us we nearly died, for in those days before fish farms and intensive production, fresh salmon was even more of a delicacy than it is now, and we could not have afforded to buy even a chunk of it without careful housekeeping.

"Even so," Mona said to me as we left the kitchen with our tails between our legs, "it'll be rotten."

It was the most wonderful taste sensation I've ever experienced.

All fish is caught seasonally, and we always arrived at the height of the salmon season, which runs from June to August, then the herring fishing starts. The salmon spawns in Irish rivers before heading off to the Sargasso Sea, the deepest part of the Atlantic, to mature. It goes through three stages of development as it grows towards adulthood, and it was in its second stage that it reached the nets of the Passage men, while a few made it through to become the big 'cock salmon' of full maturity. They called it *pale,* possibly a corruption of *peel,* but its flesh really was the palest pink, the flavour deep yet mild: the chateaubriand of the fish world. Hot or cold, with those glorious spuds or salad and mayonnaise, it was a repast fit for a king. No wonder the young Fionn Mac Cumhaill wanted to suck his thumb when he touched the side of such a fish as it turned on the spit! Our fish was a Salmon of Knowledge for me too. It taught me three very valuable things: don't knock it 'til you've tried it; don't under-estimate the kindness of neighbours; and never look a gift fish in the gills.

Other denizens of the underwater world I would have been happy to forgo, things like shellfish, that looked too much like snails for my liking, even though I was at last able to visualise what Molly Malone had on her barrow, for I'd met neither cockles nor mussels before then; and kippers, which tasted good but had so many bones that you would have needed a fleet of helicopters on standby to ferry you to the nearest bone-removal unit to have your throat stripped out, though my uncle Tom loved both. There used to be a processing plant in the village where the herring were smoked to make the kippers, but it was not there in my time.

They used to catch eels too, and as a young lad my dad would often help out with bringing the day's catch home. As the child of a merchant seaman, he was one of the few whose family did not fish for a living, though they too took their livelihood ultimately from the sea. When an eel is caught it is customary, I believe, to stun it by hitting it on the back of the head with that odd little club known as a 'priest', but if you don't do it quickly enough it wriggles up your arm and is hard to shake off. The phrase 'slippery as an eel' has its origins in close observation. In Passage the most slippery customer could be dealt with by a very simple procedure: you would draw a cross in the sand and drop the eel upon it, where it would lie still and unresisting, waiting for the *coup de grâce*.

My mother had an encounter with an eel, this time a freshwater one caught in the waters of Lough Neagh. My Granny Campbell was spending a few weeks with her sister in Ballymulderg, leaving my mother, Mona, and Wilf, home alone. They were teenagers, I suppose, and fit enough to mind themselves, but their cookery skills were none too developed at this stage of their lives. The last time they had been left to fend for themselves they had been given a chicken by a kindly neighbour, and not having the faintest idea what to do with it, decided to make soup. This involved putting the chicken into a pot, after it had been sterilised in line with Mona's stringent requirements, adding a load of vegetables and several pints of water, and boiling the whole thing for hours. The idea was to have the resulting soup for starters and the chicken for the main course, but when they went looking for their bird, it had disappeared. Of course Wilf was blamed, the girls accusing him of taking it out and hiding it 'to annoy them'. He protested his innocence, but no one would eat the soup. It wasn't until Granny arrived home that the mystery was explained. The chicken had been a very young one, and they had boiled their mess of pottage so long that the thing had dissolved away to nothing, bones and all.

A different fate was in store for the eel. Barney was an elderly man who used to visit our house to swap Westerns with Uncle Wilf. He had promised Granny that he would get her an eel whenever he could, saying it was a great delicacy, and overriding her objection that she had a very delicate stomach and would probably be unable to eat it. Barney, once set upon a course of action, was not a man to be resisted, but unfortunately he only got around to fulfilling his promise during her absence, so it was my mother who answered a knock at the door to find a cub standing there with a biscuit tin in his hands.

"Barney sent that up for Mrs. Campbell."

"What is it?"

"How do I know?"

"Open it."

"You open it." She did, and nearly died, for what she saw was a large dark snake coiled up inside.

"I'm not taking that. Away down and tell him my mother's away."

Next day, the door knocked again.

"Barney sent that up for Mrs. Campbell."

"I told you, my mother's away, and I don't want it."

"What'll I do with it?"

"Take it back, and tell him she's not here."

Day three dawned bright and clear.

"Barney sent that up for Mrs. Campbell."

By this time the eel was starting to make its presence obvious even without the tin being opened, and no one would deal with the problem. It went back and forth for over a week, for Barney could be thrawn, and whether he didn't believe my grandmother was away, or whether he thought the youngsters were making fun of him I don't know, but he wasn't going to be the one who backed down. Finally one morning they opened the door to find the tin on the step, the eel riper than ever, and my mother half-expecting to see a note stuck to the box saying, *Please look after this eel – thank you.* Wilf was bribed with a few Woodbine cigarettes and a promise not to tell Granny he was smoking to take it out the road and find a bin somewhere to dump it. God help whoever owned the bin. If you're reading this, whoever you are, please remember they were young and they were desperate.

Barney wore a gold watch and a signet ring on his left hand, and made a point of emphasising his arguments with a wave of this extremity which showed off these accoutrements to best advantage. He had worked as a young man in the west of Ireland,

and always prefaced his stories with "When I was in Castlebar…" so that I thought him a much-travelled man. Nothing ever impressed him. My mother used to say that if you told Barney you had met a man with two heads he would remember one with three whom he had encountered in Castlebar. His opinion was the definitive one, his word the last. It's fair to say he had a quare wire about himself. My mother summed up his personality thus:

"Who's like me since Leather Ass died, and Tin Ass went to America on a motor bike, except Glass Ass, and he's cracked?"

He complained that the boys at work were stealing his tools, and they probably were, because he was easy to get a rise out of, so he made himself a toolbox in which he stowed all his gear, and attached an enormous padlock. This naturally provoked a good deal of amusement, and one day when Barney was away some smart alec nailed the box to a workbench. When he came back the boys were watching to see the reaction, for Barney's temper was legendary. He tried to lift the box. He tried again. He muttered, he cursed, he finally realised what was wrong. He seized the box and wrenched it off the bench, then kicked it from one end of the workshop to the other, calling it for all the so-and-sos under the sun, telling it,

"You were never a toolbox!" Kick. "You were only an apology for a toolbox!" Kick. "I knew from the first day I made you that you were not a toolbox!" Kick, thump.

They say a bad workman quarrels with his tools. Here is the only recorded case of an angry workman quarrelling with his toolbox.

He was doing a job once in the Presbyterian church, when a man arrived at the door, which Barney had locked.

"Go away!" snarled Barney, "You can't come in till I'm finished."

"But I'm here on business," said the man, "I need to get in."

"I told you to go away!" repeated Barney, in growing annoyance.

"But I'm an elder!" begged the man. Barney glared at him.

"I don't give a damn you're a tit!" he yelled. "You're not getting in!"[9]

Back in Passage, my dad enjoyed an enduring friendship with the Baldwin family, Tom and Mary and their son John, who was one of his best mates. Tom and his brother Jim kept a couple of haulage lorries on the road, and drove the local hackney car, as well as owning a dance hall over in Woodstown. Mary often drove the taxi, and I remember thinking it very glamorous to have a female taxi-driver. Tom taught Daddy to drive, and when it was time for him to do his test he turned up, as was required, at the local Garda Station.

"You're just in time," said the Guard. "I'm going home for me tea, you can drop me round to the house."

Daddy was too polite to say no so off he went, the Guard giving him directions.

"Wait for me now, son, I'll not be long," he told him when they reached his house, and sure enough in fifteen minutes or less he was back.

"You can run me back now," he said.

When they got back to the station Daddy enquired if he could make an appointment to take his test. The Guard grinned at him.

"Come round in the morning and I'll have your licence ready for you."

After this he would occasionally do a run for Baldwin's if they were busy and that's how he met Arthur Miller.

Arthur was a middle-aged Englishman who had settled in Passage a few years earlier, and he was a buyer of fish. He would go down on the quays when the catch was being landed and select the best, then arrange for the crates to be sent up to Waterford and onwards thence to England or Dublin. He could drive but did not own a car, and would get a taxi in and out of town once a week or so to conduct his business. He took a shine to my

[9] Around Tyrone, a cow's udder is, or was, referred to as its *elder*

dad, and soon he was the preferred driver. After the business of the day was concluded he would have Daddy drive him to the Granville Hotel where he would choose a window seat, order a drink for himself and one for his companion, and say,

"Now, Patrick, let's just sit here and watch the passing parade."

Occasionally he would drive the car himself with Daddy as passenger and on one such occasion he was bowling along the road when a lad came out of nowhere on a bicycle and slammed straight into him. Arthur got out and inspected the vehicle, but this was in the days when cars were built to last, and there wasn't a mark on it that a good wash wouldn't get rid of. He turned to the boy.

"Are you hurt, son?" he asked him.

The boy was uninjured but terrified that he would get into trouble.

"No, no, I'm not hurt but I'm terrible sorry sir, I didn't see you coming."

Arthur scowled at him as he got back into the car.

"Next time I'm coming I'll send you a postcard," he promised.

John Baldwin and my dad went as far afield as Dundalk, delivering leather, and down to west Cork, at that time quite a rural and remote part of the country. It was here one night very late that they realised they were completely lost, and they looked about for a likely house at which they might ask for directions. They found a small cottage on the side of the road, and knocked, but no one came. They knocked again – and again – and finally a voice hailed them from within.

"'Tis in bed I am, so. What would oo be wantin'?"

Daddy explained their plight.

"So it's directions, is it?"

They agreed that it was.

"Which way are oo facing?"

Daddy and John exchanged glances. The voice clarified the question.

"Are oo facing easht or wesht?"

They had no idea.

"Put oor back to the door, so. Now put out oor right arm. That would be wesht. 'Tis easht oo want to go now, so take the road to oor left…"

They finally got to where they wanted to go, but more by the grace of God than through the assistance of their faceless guide.

Baldwins also kept greyhounds, generally looked after, at least in terms of feeding, by the grandmother, always known as The Ghee. When the dogs were being run my dad and John were always brought along to the meeting, and it was their job to groom the dogs and get them ready for the race on the day. A favourite ruse was to rub potín into their limbs just before the race in the belief that it made them run better. An elderly gentleman in Waterford was advised by his doctor to try the same on his arthritic legs.

"Be God I'll do that," he promised, "but do you think it would work just as well if I drank the potín and rubbed the glass over me legs?"

In Dungannon potín was not the preferred emollient. When the 'Free Scheme' was introduced the doctors were polluted by requests for prescriptions for cod liver oil. Fearing an epidemic of constipation in the area they decided to investigate, but soon discovered it was being used on the many racing greyhounds that were kept around the town. It wasn't just the doggie men who used the new National Health Service to the utmost. Mary went to the doctor one day with a veritable catalogue of ailments, and before long had a sheaf of prescriptions for all her ills.

"Just when I'm here, doctor," she said, "my Anne's not too well. I think she's run down. Could you give her something for that?"

The doctor drew another form towards him.

"And my John has no appetite, could you give me a bottle for him?" He could.

"And my Alec has pains in his knees, what about a wee rub or Sloan's lineament for that?" No problem.

"And my Kate can't get rid of her headaches… and as for my Ted…"

The long-suffering doctor signed the last form, looked at Mary and said, "Tell me madam, how are you off for sausages?"

I wonder if he knew that cat in Passage?

Some years ago we were browsing in Ballinderry Antiques when my eye fell upon a pair of pictures, one of them depicting 'The Suir at Waterford'. We bought it, at vast expense – the figure of nine pounds sterling springs to mind – because of its connection with my dad. I suppose you might describe it as naïve art. In an unkinder moment you might use other words. It looks like a child's drawing, perhaps not so accomplished, with the river sketched in a desultory fashion and a little stick-man in the foreground. The frame is also naïve, not to say rough. Not surprisingly, it is unsigned – my dad would have said the artist was ashamed to put his name to it – but there is an odd little detail, a square flapping forlornly from a railing that runs along the quay, displaying the letter 'L', that led us in a mad moment to conclude that the picture is an early Lowry, before he hit his stride with his Ancoats match stalks. Now, in even madder moments, when things look gloomy or the stipend and the outlay don't seem to be quite the same size, we are led to speculate,

"Does this mean we'll have to sell the Lowry?"

I hope not.

Buyers for such a gem might be hard to find.

Tall Ships

Tall Ship

What do a lady of doubtful reputation, and a forward player on a rugby team, have in common with a Galway fishing boat?

My dad left Passage when he was still a young man, and wound up in Birmingham where he met my mother. After I was born they came to live in Dungannon, and it was here that my dad found his spiritual home. He loved Dungannon, and he never looked back to his birthplace with anything other than affectionate remembrance, certainly not with regret. My mother liked Passage, but only as a holiday destination. It wasn't that people there didn't make you welcome, it was just that they adhered to regular meal times, with dinner at one o'clock, tea at five, supper around ten-thirty – and no drops of tea in between!

She did like their attitude to celebrity, however, for it mirrored her own. Shortly after the assassination of JFK, his widow, Jackie, who was still only Bouvier-Kennedy and hadn't yet added the Onassis, came with her children and an entourage of bodyguards and retainers to stay in Woodstown House, two miles from Passage. They gave out that because this was to be a private family holiday they desired no interruptions, and even though John-John used to steal eggs from neighbouring farms and try to sell them to the shops in Passage, their wishes were respected. Totally. So much so that three weeks into their stay they arranged a press conference and organised a dance in the village hall.

They went to Mass in Crooke chapel, just up the hill from Passage, and if you travel a few miles down the coast, you'll come to Hook Head, where there is a lighthouse. They say that when Cromwell came to Ireland he spent some time figuring out how he might conquer Waterford, and finally swore he would take it 'By Hook or by Crooke!' But the city did not yield readily to invaders, as its motto, bestowed by Henry VII, reminds us: *Urbs Intacta Manet Waterfordia*[10]; and the Lord Protector got a bit of a gunk when his siege was unsuccessful. He wasn't the first invader to take a fancy to the place, for the city had already repelled the advances of two pretenders, Lambert Simnel and Perkin Warbeck, and the Normans were here before any of them, leaving a fine memorial in Reginald's Tower, where the Norman warrior Richard de Clare, known as Strongbow, married Aoife, the daughter of the Irish Chieftain, Dermot Mac Morrough, thus forging a bond between the two traditions, and paving the way for the great Norman assimilation in which, the old history books tell us, they became 'more Irish than the Irish themselves'.

Aunt Lil wrote in my mother's autograph book, in the bottom corner of the last page: 'By Hook or by Crooke I'll be last in your book!' John Baston added in minute lettering down on the very binding of the little volume: 'I'll be damned if you will, Auntie Lil!'

Daddy was in Twomey's pub one night when the crack came round to burials. One man held that since there was no afterlife, it didn't matter where your mortal remains ended up.

---

[10] *Waterford remains the untaken city*

"When you're dead, you're dead, like our dog Flora."

Another, who had delusions of patriotism, if not of grandeur, instructed the assembled company,

"If anything happens to me, just stick the green and gold up me arse and float me out the creek."

But one man there gave it a bit more thought. "I'd like to lie somewhere where the Hook light can shine on me," he said.

My dad retained a lifelong fondness for the sea and anything to do with it. It was even with him in dreams! He always talked in his sleep, usually muttering odd words and phrases connected with work, but one night my mum woke to find him dipping in and out of bed with a peculiar lifting motion.

"What on earth are you doing, Pat?" she enquired, with some asperity, before she realised he was still fast asleep.

"Hauling it up on its bed," he informed her solemnly, eyes tight shut.

"Hauling what up on its bed?" she demanded, exasperated.

He smiled, as one well satisfied with his work. "The Mediterranean," he told her.

The sea claimed the life of my grandfather D'Arcy, who was in the merchant navy during the war. The cargo ship he worked on plied between England and Australia, and had just docked in Liverpool when the city suffered an aerial bombardment. He was due to go home on leave, so when a muster roll was called, his absence was attributed to his being on furlough, and it was only when he failed to return after two weeks that questions began to be asked. The authorities contacted his family, established that he hadn't been home, and finally he was officially listed as missing.

My dad's brother Tom, then in the Irish army, was heading home when he met a neighbour. She had heard the news before him, and stopped to sympathise, but Tom thought she was speaking of his grandfather, who had died only weeks before. As the confusion became clear, she said gently,

"You don't know, do you son?"

———— ∞ ————

"Know what?" asked Tom.

"That your father is missing," she said.

As he came on into Passage he met Mary Baldwin in her hackney car. Her passenger was a Captain Murray, an official with the cross-channel shipping companies, and it was he who set things in motion for the dredging of the dock, where, after some days, the body was recovered. The verdict was that he had been blown off deck by the force of the blasts, and drowned in the quay. Oddly enough, it was 1941, the same year my mother's father died in America.

Despite this, as I say, my dad loved the sea, and it was in recognition of this that I arranged to take him to Scotland, shortly after my mother's death, to see the Tall Ships.

The Tall Ships race is one of the most gorgeous spectacles you will ever see, the grace, beauty, and sheer magnificence of these wonderful vessels guaranteed to stop you in your tracks as surely as Valentin Iremonger's *ground glass under a door.*[11] They had been to Belfast a couple of years before and we tried to see them there, but we completely underestimated their popularity and got stuck in a traffic grid-lock such as the M25 might be proud of, arriving just in time to see the last sail dip below the horizon – romantic, but not very satisfactory. So it was with great excitement that we set off from Belfast on an Ulsterbus tour bound for Glasgow, where we would stay in the Central Hotel, heading thence the next morning by bus to Leith, there to see the ships at close range and mingle with like-minded folk, and if we were lucky, one or two crew members. The journey was pleasant if uneventful, but marked for me by the worst sore throat I've ever had and an overdose of Lem-sips and Strepsils.

We arrived at the Central Hotel, a slightly faded remnant of the great days of Edwardian splendour, in pouring rain, but determined not to be as downcast as the skies. Twenty minutes later there was no sign of our being allowed to get off the bus,

---

[11] *Spring Jag* by Valentin Iremonger

———————

and there was much speculation coupled with craning of necks and discontented murmuring. Finally our courier came back to tell us that the management was very sorry for the delay but the hotel was on fire and did we mind waiting a bit longer? With the good nature normally associated with the people of our wee province, we readily agreed to wait until the flames were extinguished before being assigned our rooms.

At this time my dad's hearing was very poor, and he was showing the first signs of the Alzheimer's that would later destroy him, though I did not recognise it as such. But I knew he was a bit forgetful, a bit uncertain, and I had requested that we be given a twin room so that I could keep an eye on him, make sure he knew where he was, and where he was going. They gave us a double. I took myself down to reception where, after a deal of kerfuffling, they informed me they didn't have a twin room left, but if we would go and have tea somewhere they would find twin beds and rearrange things more or less as I had requested. My dad, God bless him, informed me with great courtesy that he didn't mind where he slept and the floor would do for him! I thought otherwise.

We headed out in search of food and I found a cosy Italian restaurant, which he loved. Always a fan of good food in nice surroundings, he had never eaten in an authentic Italian place before, so he was in his element. The waiter was delightful, taking Daddy under his wing and looking after him like his long-lost uncle. He described the food, discussed the wine, explained what went into the desserts, and we had a grand time. In all my life I have only seen Daddy really narked when he was hungry; feed him, and he was a pussycat. He suffered for years from a duodenal ulcer until a bottle from Tommy Lee in Portadown cured him, and it may have been this condition which made it essential for him to have some form of sustenance at regular intervals. The Campbells never cared when they ate, but continual drops of tea were necessary to their very existence.

The Italian experience tucked under our belts, we returned to find the room rearranged to my satisfaction, the only problem now being that the en-suite bathroom had one of those old-fashioned tubs with brass taps, and the cold one dripped all night. Gushed might be a more accurate description, and the door didn't close properly. I decided it was wiser to say nothing. Daddy slept like a baby, but my bed was next to the bathroom. It was like camping beside Niagara Falls. I finally fell asleep through sheer exhaustion, perhaps hypnotised by the steady drip, only to be wakened by an ear-shattering ringing at about three in the morning, that curious time between night and day when you know that try as you might you will never be able to drop off again. I was too annoyed to be afraid, so I merely groped for the phone and dialled Reception.

"Do we have to evacuate the building?" I enquired with great civility.

Not at all, not at all, I was assured, it was just something in the kitchen that had set off the smoke alarms, which were connected to the fire alarms... The following morning it occurred to me that I should have asked *what* had set off the smoke alarms, but since we hadn't been burned in our beds it seemed churlish, if not a trifle precious, to pursue the matter. It reminded me of an incident that happened to a cousin of mine when he was staying in digs in Magherafelt. He arrived home one night to see smoke filtering out under the door of another lodger's room, and he burst in to find the bedclothes well alight and the man sound asleep. The only thing that saved him was that the bedding was made of some kind of synthetic fabric which, instead of blazing up, was melting away in curls onto the floor. Nonetheless Dick woke the man and doused the bed with water, and soon everything was back to normal.

"I suppose you were smoking in bed," admonished Dick. "Well, let that be a lesson to you."

"Och, I wouldn't worry," the other replied calmly, "though I'm grateful for your help. But whatever kind of a boyo I am, fire doesn't do me no harm."

The next day's sojourn among the Tall Ships at the pier of Leith made up for all the irritations of the previous one. It was a humbling yet uplifting experience, and we came back to the hotel in fine form, ready to admit that it was, in fact, a very decent establishment, give or take a few minor inconveniences like fire and flood. That evening as we were looking for somewhere to eat I came across an advertisement for a restaurant called The Ubiquitous Chip, and I had a vague recollection that I had read a good account of it somewhere, so off we went to the other side of Glasgow in search of it. It was as good as I hoped it would be, tucked away in a little hidden courtyard, encased in glass walls covered by massive vines and ivies, romanticised by subtle lighting, where the cobbles of the street wandered in to form the floor. The food was superb – they don't actually serve chips! – from the chilled summer fruit soup decorated with crystallised rose petals to the Aberdeen Angus steaks with wholegrain mustard, and the sweet menu was to die for. But the Muscat dessert wine almost finished me off. I have never been drunk in my life, and I say this not in any self-righteous way but merely as a statement of fact, but I forgot about the Strepsils I had been popping all day, my throat still feeling like sandpaper after a close encounter with a railway sleeper. The sweet mellow beverage mingled with the soothing balm of those little diskettes produced an effect which, if you could package it, would make you a fortune round the clubs of London. I vaguely remember getting a taxi back to the hotel. I dimly recall phoning home where my friend Issy and her sister were baby-sitting my house and my dog, and her incredulous question, "Aideen, are you drunk?" I am sure I said no, but I know I was, for the dripping tap sounded like music to my ears and I even forgot to say goodnight to the dog.

The journey down to Stranraer next afternoon saw everyone in high good spirits. We were bowling along a good wide stretch of road in the competent hands of our driver Richard, the courier Eileen had just told us we were thirty minutes or so from the docks, and I bent to get another Strepsil from my bag. I was aware of a dull thud, and bits of what looked like rubber fly-ing past the window as I glanced up. I thought we had had a blow-out. Then I realised that the bus was heading at breakneck speed for the crash barrier on the other side of the road where the ground fell away steeply for several hundred feet. Before I had fully grasped the implications of this, we hit the barrier side on and travelled along it for a couple of hundred yards, finally com-ing to a juddering halt, still, thankfully, on the road, but only by the grace of God and our driver's presence of mind. Then I noticed that the steps leading up to the door into the coach and the rail on which Eileen's feet had been resting seconds before had been ripped clean away, but fortunately she had begun to gather her things together and had pulled her feet back under her own seat a fraction of time earlier. Her shoes had disappeared.

There was no panic. Everyone got out through the emer-gency exit and we began to piece together what had happened. Passengers near the front reported seeing a VW Passat coming out of a side road to our left, almost under the wheels of the bus. Richard had swerved to avoid it and been forced across the road into the path of an oncoming car. The Passat was driven by a Dutchman, over on holiday, and it might have been a case of mistaken priorities, but who can say? A moment's lapse, a misunderstanding, but two people in the other car died that day, two people travelling along a good road, in clear daylight, doing nothing wrong, completely, totally, and utterly blameless; and if it hadn't been for the skill and courage of our driver, there might have been many more.

There was a male nurse and a doctor on board, but the people in the car were beyond help. Another car stopped, the driver also a nurse, and soon the emergency services arrived, followed by a group of ladies from some organisation like the WI who brought us tea and sandwiches, for the bus was out of commission and we had to sit there until a replacement could be found to take us the last few miles to the boat. Needless to say we missed our sailing, and they held up the last departure of the night for us. Mobile phones were much less common than they are now, but one man handed his phone round to anyone who wanted it, and refused absolutely to accept any recompense for the calls. I rang Issy.

"Am I glad to hear from you!" she spluttered as we connected. "We've had a bit of a problem here…"

"Don't panic," I cut across her, "but we've been involved in a bit of an accident…"

God bless Northern Ireland understatement! She didn't tell me until she picked us up in Belfast that the boiler had burst, and only the timely assistance of our good friend Frank Doran, always there in a crisis, had avoided having the whole house flooded for our return.

The Walrus and the Carpenter wanted to talk of shoes and ships and sealing wax, of cabbages and kings, but we only wanted to talk about the ships – *The Asgard, The Tradewind, The Gallant, Fair Jeanne, Mist of Avalon, Esmeralda* – and forget how horribly the whole trip had ended. But human beings are resilient, as they must be, if we are to live our lives without becoming completely weighed down by the sadness we encounter every day, and soon our minds were filled again with the Tall Ships, their white wings blotting out the horror and the darkness.

The following Christmas, Issy bought my dad a model of a Galway fishing boat, cunningly wrought, complete in every detail down to the coils of rope on the deck and the little crates for the fish. She added tiny figurines of an old sea captain and two sailor men, and a ship's cat, for although sailors don't actually like cats at sea, they are good for keeping the rats and mice down, and you must never put one off if it stows away! The boat sits in front of me now as I write, with its two sails of unbleached linen and one of saffron, its sleek outline hinting at latent power, ready to take on the worst the sea can throw at it, *The Queen of Connemara* in miniscule, a beauty in every line.

In the last few months he spent at home, my dad's sleep patterns became increasingly irregular. For a man who had always fallen asleep as soon as he hit the pillow, and wakened in or around six-thirty and not a minute before, this was hard to get used to, and very distressing. He told us that now, when he woke in the morning, too early to get up, he would lie and look at the boat, loving to watch it in the dawn light, coming into sharper and clearer focus as the sun rode up the sky.

I wonder what thoughts went through his mind then? Was he back in Passage, helping Arthur Miller choose the best of the fish, swimming off the breakwater with his dog, Bing, or being ferried to Ballyhack by Patsy Barron, the only man I ever knew who had a real wooden leg? Was he sad that there is now a proper car ferry instead of Patsy's wee boat with the outboard motor? Did he think about Moll, or The Ghee, or the passing parade? Did he see mares' tails?

Sometimes, if you caught my dad in a brown study and offered him 'a penny for them,' he would smile and say,

"Och, thoughts that do be crossing the mind."

Maybe on those mornings he just entrusted his thoughts to the old boat's keeping, and let the sea take them where it would…and remembered that a Galway fishing boat is known as a Hooker.

A Child Twice (for Pat)

You left your cap hanging on the back of the door.

The last time I saw you wear it
I wondered why you didn't move out of the sun,
But sat in your chair and let your forehead burn.

I was cross, because I thought you thrawn.

Now I know your mind could not retain
The things I knew you knew, and always had.
The things that made you, you,
And then made me.

As well try to carry water in a sieve,
Or bind the ocean with a twist of straw.

Tights and Teddy Bears

A dear friend, Mrs. Fahy

I never paid much attention to the nursery rhyme, *The Teddy Bears' Picnic,* when I was a child, but that was because I little knew that I would one day ride in a taxi with some of its participants. It wasn't just any taxi. It was the minibus owned by our good friend Raymond which used to ferry mum and dad, Posy and me, and as motley a crew as you could find anywhere, to the eleven o'clock Mass on a Sunday morning.

The teddy bears were masquerading as three elderly ladies, two of whom wore mink, and who resolutely occupied a full double seat each, lest anyone should inadvertently crease a hair of the luxurious pelt – the mink's, not theirs. Mink hats adorned their carefully coiffed heads. The third lady had what in my teenage years was referred to as a 'fun fur', purely, I believe, to avoid the contumely of 'fake fur'. But fake it most certainly was. It lacked the lustre, the sheen, the cachet of the other two. It was dull, lifeless, and quite clearly had never been on any creature other than the one it now adorned, in the double seat it was happy to share

———— ∞ ————

with anyone who cared to sit beside it. For me it was infinitely preferable to its more expensive brethren, but it also sported, as if it were conscious of its inferior status and wished either to make up for it or thumb its nose, a bunch of plastic fruit in its lapel. Of the other two, one had a roll collar and needed no embellishment, the other was smooth and unadorned.

I had been travelling in the minibus since I was tiny, but oddly no one ever noticed that I was growing up, indeed that I had reached adulthood, graduated, and gone to work as a librarian in the far-off realms of Craigavon. There was good reason for this negation of the obvious. If ever there was an extra passenger, which was quite acceptable since our merry band of regulars did not reach capacity load, there was a general cry of "Aideen can share/sit on someone's knee/squeeze in!" And there was always the jump seat.

The alternative would have been for the minks to double up. Perhaps the tendency of the critters to breed like rabbits was embedded in the ladies' psyche, though I think they only do it with their own kind, but they were taking no chances. Many a bumpy ride I enjoyed en route to Saint Patrick's, but since the journey was not long, and I was going to pray, and my mother would have killed me if I had said anything, I bore it stoically. It was character-building.

Their other great fear, besides crushing, was incineration. Nearly everyone smoked then, and Freddie used to wait until the homeward leg, for no one would smoke going to church, before offering his cigarettes all round. Mum and Mona always partook, Mink 1 and Mink 2 were abstemious, and Bunch of Fruit always said the same thing:

"I don't smoke… well, I do smoke… but I nivver smoke after Communion till I get three sips of water down my throat."

At this Freddie would share a secret smile with our party and gallantly light up the ladies' before his own. The minks withdrew as far as possible into their seats, for both were ladies of stature, and stuck their noses in the air.

Bunch of Fruit had a tremulous voice that constantly seemed on the verge of failing her, but it never did. She was a warm, kindly, genuine woman, totally without pretension, and used to tell us of the All Souls' Night she got rather more than she bargained for when she put out the plate of bread and the glass of water, in case any of the souls who were rambling about should fancy nipping in for a quick snack. I wonder if anyone does that now? We used to do it in the old days, but we stopped after Wilf got up in the wee small hours to take a tablet for the toothache, and helped himself from the glass that stood on the table rather than walk the extra few yards to the sink. It wasn't his lack of courtesy that stopped the practice; it was Mona's near hysterics the following morning when she found the glass moved and the contents depleted by nearly two-thirds.

When Bunch of Fruit came down to her kitchen, it wasn't the glass that had been tampered with.

"Missus," she told mum with perfect seriousness, "the Holy Souls had been at the bread. They didn't eat it all, but the track of their teeth was in the bits that were left on the plate."

My mother's comment that it was comforting to know you still had your teeth in the afterlife was met with stony silence.

Freddie was the first to be dropped off on the return journey, and again this was the cue for a ritual pronouncement. As soon as his foot hit the step prior to descent, Fruit would take in the rest of us with a sweep of the hand and a glance at his departing back.

"He's a credit," she would say invariably, and as she had said for the last God knows how many years, as if he were totally deaf or incapable of understanding what she was saying. "He was near dead a lock a years ago, and look at him now."

Again he would share a last smile with my mum, and head down the path with a wave of his hand, not looking back.

Raymond taxied us everywhere for years until the Troubles got really bad and he didn't like to be abroad at night. Then we went to John Hughes.

———— ∽ ————

In those days we didn't have a telephone; neither, of course, did we have a car, but we did have a standing arrangement with the Fahy family, to visit each other on alternate Friday nights. John would collect whoever was out and about and ferry us home. His instruction was always the same: "Lift us at D'Arcy's/Fahy's and leave us till the last."

One night when I was in Dublin, mum and Mona set out on their trek to the White City, where the Fahys lived. It was a good wee walk, and all uphill, but they were well used to it. This evening, however, it was pelting with rain, and they hadn't gone far before they realised they would be well and truly soaked before they were even halfway there. At the foot of the Donaghmore Road they took a rain check – literally. At this time we were living in Ballysaggart, and our route to the White City was along the Newell Road, up the Quarry Lane, down past the hospital, along Altmore Drive and into Bernagh Gardens. John lived up the Donaghmore Road, definitely not on the flight path, but the girls hit on a plan. Why not walk up to his house and get him to run them the rest of the way? That would be a shorter walk, and a better option. They toiled up the hill, their mood not improved by the weight of the stack of magazines they had decided to bring with them and which were now sopping wet and growing heavier by the minute, then swiftly turning murderous when it turned out that John was out on a run, and there was no taxi to be had at that time.

Campbells, however, are made of stern stuff. They might not have had the great Argyll going before, but determined as they were not to let a drop of rain spoil their night, they soldiered on. As they stood waiting to cross the road at the Sprickley Well, Mona turned to mum and advised,

"Stand in as the cars pass for they're liable to splash us."

My mother looked at the speaker, drenched from head to foot, hair dripping, shoes squelching, raindrops sliding down her nose, and asked the obvious question:

"Are we mad?"

A quick confab decided them: madness was definitely the only possible excuse for finishing such a journey, and even though Voltaire has remarked that to be mad is not easy, they had nothing more to prove, so they turned for home. As they reached the final furlong, a thought struck them. John would be arriving as usual after all his other runs were over to collect them at Fahy's and that wouldn't be right; he must be advised of the change of plan. So they detoured once more up the Donaghmore Road, cancelled their taxi, and swam home. Their account ended here when I got to hear of it, but my dad took up the story.

"I was minding my own business having a quiet read at the paper, thinking that the two girls were mad to head out on a night like that when the door burst open. In they came shaking themselves like dogs, and a bundle of wet papers hit the deck. Then I had to dive for cover. Coats went one way, shoes another. Tights whizzed past me, one pair that way, one pair this; skirts and blouses flew through the air – I was afraid to guess what would be next. Every chair back was festooned with a piece of clothing. I didn't know where to look. Next thing I see is them diving up the stairs, coming back wrapped in towels, and the steam rising out of them. They were like two drowned rats. I set down the paper. "'Is it raining?' says I."

He didn't have to add the bit about mum rolling her eyes with a droll look at her sister. I could picture that for myself. And hear her comment.

"Turn the fire up, Pat. And put the kettle on."

Love among the Whins

Patrick, Maureen and Aideen

"But where is he? I need to get home, my mother'll kill me. And for that matter where's Anna?"

Anna was always in love, but not always with the same person. Her mother actively promoted the claims of Tim because he had money, but Anna wanted Romance, and would have none of him. It was love or nothing. She believed in the advice given by an old lady who warned her, "Marry for love and work for money, not the other way round", but if love is blind, then Anna was at best short-sighted, and her choices were often more attractive in her over-active imagination than they were in reality.

The current squeeze, Eddie, had invited Anna to a ceilidh house above Carrickmore whose owner was said to be an accomplished fiddler, so they could be sure of a good night's crack. She invited my mother and, I think, Gogga Rice, along with Francie, a good friend of ours, to make up a party, and off they went, Eddie driving, with Anna in the front seat so they could make sheep's eyes at each other, the other three squeezed into the back.

Their destination proved to be a huxter in the hills, miles from anywhere, none too clean, and occupied by a couple of brothers whose idea of crack was to sit on opposite sides of the fire seeing how far each one could spit. Tea was readily offered and as readily refused, and a fiddle might have been produced, but in due course Anna and Eddie withdrew to walk in the moonlight and count the stars. The rest of them made the best of the situation but time wore on, and it's a good drive back to Dungannon. My mother knew she would get a rollicking from Granny Campbell if she was too late, and she began to get restless. I suspect she was also bored! Gogga went to the door and looked about but there was no sign of the lovers. Finally Anna arrived back in a daze, dreamily announcing that she had left Eddie somewhere in the hills, broken-hearted because she had told him she wouldn't marry him. She sat down by the fire with a rapturous expression on her face straight out of Hollywood, while my mother dispatched Francie to find the driver. A short while later Francie returned alone, but not entirely unsuccessful.

"Maureen, you may come and talk to this eejit. I found him clocking like an oul' hen among the whins and he says he's going nowhere until Anna says she'll marry him."

It took all my mother's powers of persuasion, and she had many, to force him to come back to the house, and another twenty minutes or so before he would consent to drive them home. He threatened suicide, and mum told him in no uncertain terms that he could do whatever he pleased as soon as she was dropped off on the Donaghmore Road but not before. Eventually they piled into the car with great relief, and he drove like a man possessed, the only thing he didn't knock down being something that wasn't there. As they swung into Donaghmore he revived sufficiently to ask, "Are we through Pomeroy yet?"

Despite experiences such as this, my mother continued to be a confidante for Anna. It was Anna who owned the salon that never shut, and her mother, a taut little madam who could clip straws with her ass, used to pop in and out to make sure the girl wasn't up to any mischief. One day my mother spotted her approaching and called a warning to Anna, who was entertaining a beau in the back of the shop. He couldn't get out, so Mum rushed in and stuck him under the dryer, threw a robe over him and handed him a magazine while Anna went out to decoy her mother. Mrs. Cassidy chatted for a few minutes then prepared to leave. At the door she turned and beckoned my mother over.

"Maureen? It shouldn't take the short hair long to dry."

One of Anna's longest running affairs was with Paul, who worked in a shop in town. One day Mrs. Cassidy was making her progress down the street when she saw him adjusting a display in the window. Meeting my mother later she told her,

"I was about to go in and ask them the price of the monkey."

My mother wasn't impressed by his appearance either, but loyalty to Anna kept her quiet. She told Gogga later, however, that in her opinion, they had spoiled a good monkey when they cut the tail off.

Anna discovered *Wuthering Heights* during this period, and immediately became captivated by it – obsessed is nearer the mark. She began to refer to herself as *Cathy*, insisted that she would die in Spring, and wrote letters to Paul calling him *My darling Heathcliff,* while he responded in kind. Who can say that it was not her experiences on the wild moorland above Carrickmore that sparked such a violent reaction? Mona was incensed at what she considered to be an adulteration of one of her favourite books, and unlike my mother, refused to see the funny side.

My mother always believed there was a genuine fondness between Anna and Paul, but parental influence is strong, and eventually Anna decided to end it. Paul turned up at our house to pour out his heart to my mum, keeping her standing at the door for hours while he regaled her with details of his broken heart. She was young and perhaps a trifle unsympathetic, but the recital embarrassed and irritated her. My family was never given to public displays of affection, and always had a sneaking suspicion that such a parade of emotion was not genuine. At last she managed to get a word in edgeways and advised him that he should accept Anna's decision and move on, but he clutched at her dramatically, fell to his knees on the doorstep, and cried out,

"But Jesus, I love her!" It was a favourite catchphrase of ours for years.

Love, according to some, is an itching at the heart that you can't scratch. To my none-too-romantic mother, it was a trickle down your back that you can't lick, and she never trusted men who were too flowery in their addresses. 'Oul' plamass,' she called it, and as Gogga once said to a handsome GI who was sweet-talking her at a dance,

"Your line isn't long enough, and your bait isn't strong enough, to catch the Irish fish."

Gogga was never stuck for a riposte in any situation. She was in Cassie O'Neill's shop one day when an American visitor came in. Cassie asked him how he was enjoying his holiday and he said, well enough, but there wasn't much to be said for the local women.

"Take my Mom," he boasted. "Sometimes I take her out for the evening, wine and dine her and take her dancing. All the guys are queuing up to cut in and take her round the floor. She could knock any of the girls I've met in Dungannon into a cocked baseball hat."

Cassie was furious, but Gogga smiled.

"Isn't that marvellous!" she enthused. "Dining and dancing! What a goer – and her son well nigh past it himself."

The man was probably not the real alley-daly when it came to Americans, but more likely a 'returned American', one of a breed that occupied a high place in Gogga's – and my mother's – canon of contemptibles.

The phrase denoted someone who had been away from home for a short period and came back more Yankee that the Yanks, or in some cases more British than the Brits, but the condition was the same no matter where the place of temporary residence might have been. It had two major symptoms: an acquired accent, which Daddy described as 'bastard Kilmacow'; and a tendency to forget everything about the homeland, or worse, to treat it with disdain. The accent, my mother was quick to note, was unusual in several respects. Firstly, it varied little according to where the speaker had been, so that a returned American who had spent time in Texas would sound exactly the same as one who had never set foot outside The Bronx; similarly, you would have been hard put to decide whether a returnee from the UK had worked in the Austin in Birmingham, or on the coaly Tyne. Secondly, those who were afflicted only had to be away for a brief period for the linguistic metamorphosis to be complete, but no matter how long they stayed at home, they never regained their Northern Ireland lilt. I had a friend who, like many of my school mates, went off to the States for the summer after her 'A' levels, but when the ship docked in New York, she got cold feet and stayed only long enough to arrange her passage home by the return sailing. She didn't even have time to buy miniature Statues of Liberty for the folks back home, but she did acquire a stonking American twang.

It wasn't only in the USA and England that the malady could be caught. When I was living in Dublin I introduced my mother to a fellow student whom we met at a bus stop, explaining that she had just come up into College that very term. They chatted for a while and mum enquired where she was from – might it be The Liberties, Sheriff Street, The Monto?

"Ah, no," she replied in a voice that would have done Biddy Mulligan proud. "I'm from The Moy."

This refusal to accept your birthright was seen as an insult to your forbears, and my mother was fond of quoting,

> *The stranger's jeer I do not fear, but can I pardon ever*
> *He who reviles his native isle? Oh, never, never, never!*

Or in loftier moments, when only Scott would do:

---◇◇◇---

Breathes there a man with soul so dead
Who never to himself hath said,
'This is my own, my native land?'

There were many, alas, who were only too happy to erase all memories of a previous existence, like the man who enquired in a pronounced nasal drawl, "Is that the cat that was a kitten when I was back home?" Or the girl who, arrived in Magherafelt after a sojourn in the Big Apple, got a taxi out to the home place. When they drew up at her parents' house she registered great surprise and cried,

"Hey, I don't remember the place being so small!"

Her driver turned to her. "Wouldn't you wonder at that now, and the track of your bare feet still in the dunghill at the back dure."

It was definitely a man of similar sensibilities who was whiling away a summer evening smoking his pipe, leaning on a gate and watching the world go by, when a smart car drew up beside him.

"Which of these roads shall I take for Dungannon?" drawled the driver, a young man known to the smoker as one who had left the area barely a year before. He took the pipe from his mouth and tapped it thoughtfully on his hand before replying.

"Divil the hate I care, son, they're all one to me."

My mother detested any form of pretension, and wasn't behind any door when it came to the put-down. She was forced to listen one night as a man held forth at great length upon a subject which he clearly knew nothing about, but who was carried away by the force of his own argument. No one could get a word in edgeways, until finally he had to draw breath and someone turned to my mum.

"What do you think, Maureen?" She considered a moment.

"Me?" she said sweetly. "I always think that it's better to be quiet and thought a fool than to speak and remove the doubt."

Gogga would have approved of that, as she would of the reply a friend of mine gave to a guy who was chatting her up at a disco.

"I'd love to dance with you," he told her, "but I have nowhere to put my Porsche keys. Would they fit in your bag?"

"Why don't you put them in your mouth?" she suggested.

Veronica – aka Gogga – was a very striking girl, with an abundance of black hair, and absolutely no vanity about her appearance. She called herself 'The Baby', or else someone bestowed that soubriquet on her, and one of her favourite pastimes was playing Long Donkey with Uncle Wilf. One night she arranged to meet Mona up town to introduce her latest date. Next day she asked Mona her opinion of him.

"I couldn't see him very well in the dark, Veronica," Mona replied truthfully.

Gogga gave a shout of laughter. "Why do you think I wanted you to meet him at night? He has eyes in his forehead like a horse. You know the kind The Baby gets!"

When Mona related this tale to my mother she replied, laughing,

"And she was right. I met him, and he's a tragedy in pants."

Gogga was very straight, a quality that much appealed to Mona, and could always be relied on in a crisis. One night Mona had agreed to meet someone to go to the pictures but chickened out, and asked Veronica to make her excuses. A few days later Mona was in Dynes's ice-cream parlour when in walked her would-be date. He approached solemnly and offered his condolences, sat down and chatted quietly with none of his accustomed verve or humour. Mona was at a loss until Gogga arrived.

"Excuse me," she said sweetly. "Could I just have a word with my friend?"

Taking Mona aside she explained,

"I told yer man your great-aunt died, that's why you couldn't go to the pictures. I didn't want to make it any closer otherwise you wouldn't have been able to go anywhere for a week. This way you don't even need to be too sorry about her."

My mother was working as a hairdresser in Coagh, and she came home one evening feeling wretched. Her throat ached, her

———— ✺ ————

eyes watered, and her head was splitting. As a victim of migraine, any illness was likely to trigger an attack and so it was now. She felt like a graveyard relic. In came Veronica.

"I think I'm taking the flu," mum told her.

"Our Joe has great tablets," Veronica said. "He swears by them. Houl' on a minute and I'll get you a couple."

She was back in a trice with two large flat tablets which my mother seized and swallowed before you could say Mrs. Cullen's Powder, for she would have tried anything to get rid of a headache, and many's the concoction she sampled in her lifetime. She took herself off to bed and Veronica went home.

Mum woke in the morning feeling like a million dollars. Gone were the shivers, gone the sore throat, and gone the headache, and when you consider that a migraine attack often lasted her for three days, this was quite a result. She headed off to work, on the seven forty-five bus from The Square in Dungannon to Hanover Square in Coagh. At about eight o'clock Gogga called on my grandmother.

"Where's Maureen?"

"Gone to work, Veronica."

"How is she?" she enquired, her face full of concern.

"Absolutely fine."

For the rest of the day, Gogga was in and out of the house like something demented, asking was mum home, was there any word from her, until Granny asked her if *she* was all right. My mum got home about six-thirty, unless she called in with Patsy Sally or Mrs. McCrystal on the way, and today she hadn't her backside to the chair until Gogga appeared at the door, looking strained and anxious.

"Are you all right, Campbell?"

"Never better," mum confirmed. "Those are great tablets, Veronica, I must get the name of them from you."

Gogga was looking everywhere but at her. "Well, about those tablets…"

The tablets were veterinary ones that her brother Joe, a cattle dealer, had got for the animals. Gogga had lifted them in mistake for the ones she intended to bring, and the realisation brought with it a horror that her best friend might be poisoned. When my mother stopped laughing, and Granny finally understood what had kept Gogga on eggs all day, mum asked her,

"What were you worried about, Veronica? Did you expect me to come home roaring?"

The friendship with Veronica dated back to schooldays, when she and mum used to walk down to the Academy together, where they used to enjoy a sneaky smoke. Veronica would pinch a cigarette and a couple of matches from one of her older brothers, then during class ask out to the loo. Coming back, she would ask to speak to her pal, Maureen.

"There's a wee butt on the window in the toilet."

Seconds later, mum would ask, "May I leave the room, please?" and finish the cigarette that had been left burning on the sill.

Once they were rumbled by a classmate who told Miss Noone, a teacher of the old school, known for her sarcastic comments, like the time she felt that my mum was displaying too much personality and remarked as she walked away from her desk after picking up her corrected exercise book, "There goes Greta Garbo."

She probably knew all about the clandestine smokes but did nothing about it until it was brought to her attention, when the girls got told off. They were furious, and determined to have their revenge. They followed the informer up to the toilets, and when they judged that she would be in position they crept along outside, until they came to the window of the cubicle she was in. Fortunately, or not, depending on where you're coming from, it was slightly open. Gogga slipped in her hand and pulled the chain.

Gogga possessed a brilliant mathematical mind but had no interest in anything literary or historical. But we all of us have our fifteen minutes of fame, and Gogga's came on the day of the General Inspection.

———— ∞ ————

The nuns were keen to showcase their best pupils, and used the not very subtle method of putting the weaker ones in the back row and the strong ones in the front, so that Gogga might be to the fore when it came to mental arithmetic, but my mum would be in the van for oral English. The inspector who came for the English exam was cold and distant, and his approach was to point at a pupil and drawl, "Something from Shakespeare… something from Tennyson," usually letting the child say about three lines before jumping to someone else, so that everybody was edgy. He buttonholed Gogga and demanded, "Some historical ballad."

Reverend Mother at the front of the class closed her eyes, no doubt to pray, while my mother sent silent vibes to her pal, willing her to think of something. But she was up to the challenge.

"Who fears to speak of '98?" she declaimed, *"Who blushes at the name? When cowards mock the patriot's fate, Who hangs his head for shame?"*

Reverend Mother nearly fainted, recognising a patriotic ballad when she heard one, and terrified lest she might be suspected of having taught it, for in those days Irish history and Irish poetry were barred from the curriculum. She signalled frantically to Veronica to change course, or better still, to stop, in case she would cause offence, but Gogga thought she was being encouraged and got more and more forceful with each verse. The inspector let her finish the entire poem, while the rest of the class sat with heads bowed in mortification.

For years she came and went in our house as easily as in her own, part of the family, an honorary sister, and one night she called as usual and sat until the wee small hours of the morning, chatting away. She got up to go, said good night and when she got as far as the top of the stairs that led from the basement kitchen to the front door she called back,

"By the way, girls, I'm off to New York in the morning."

She never wrote, or sent a Christmas card, and they didn't see her again for maybe twenty years.

———————

Dancing and Lunacy

Patsy Bloomfield, in 'Showboat'

"Hairy Mary, hairy Lizzie, and all the hairy family! Every time you touch, toss, or tumble toes you get a graaaaand cigar! Hit her on the belly and she'll fall back!"

No, it's not some obscene or offensive shorthand, it's what the man who operated the coconut shy used to call out to potential customers as they made their way around the competing attractions of the funfair that came annually to Hales's field. It had changed little between my mum's day and mine, and we both enjoyed the dodgems, the roundabout and the swing-boats, the lights and the music. It's hard to imagine now how this type of entertainment could evoke such excitement in the neighbourhood, and not just from the kids. But when you didn't travel down to Newcastle or up to Portrush every weekend, or Marbella every summer, candy-floss was a rare treat. I don't know anybody who actually likes eating the stuff, but we all love to watch it being made!

The circus, too, was a big attraction, and knowing nothing then about cruelty to animals or exploitation, it really was a case of ignorance being bliss. I had been in love with circuses ever since I saw the movie *The Greatest Show on Earth,* my only problem being that nothing that came to Dungannon ever matched up to the Hollywood version – *quelle surprise!* Wilf was very taken with the circus too, so much so that he ran off with one, and wasn't spotted – or missed – until the wagons were about two miles up the Donaghmore Road, and someone had to fall out and bring him home.

I once asked an old school friend if she was dating anyone special.

"Och, you know me," she replied. "A night here and a night there, like Duffy's circus."

My childhood vocabulary did not contain the word 'bored', and it would have been quickly dismissed if I had tried to include it: "When I was your age I didn't know there was such a word. Away and play yourself," being the likely response. There's a saying that some people could enjoy themselves sitting on a wall, and that's exactly what many folk did. The kids congregated round the backs of the houses, and might line up along a gate or the wall at the top of Charlemont Street, chewing penny bubblies till our jaws got tired, or bashing chunks of Highland Toffee against the wall to break it, so that we could share it out. There might have been a bike or two to take turns on, for we didn't have one each, or we might have played *Do, Dare, Promise or Repeat* if we were tired of more energetic pursuits. The women stood around the doors or dandered over to the shop, then as the night drew in, dropped in to each other's houses or got out the sewing. The men took a walk up town, where they might come across a group of lads playing football in Irish Street with rolled-up newspaper balls.

Entertainment came largely from other people, and there was always the pictures. I remember The Castle and The Astor cinemas, and I think there was another one, possibly The Viceroy, but that might have been a ballroom. Films were shown in the

Foresters' Hall on the Donaghmore Road but that had disappeared long before my time. It didn't stop Wilf from claiming to have seen every film 'forty years ago in the oul Foresters' Hall', even though that would have meant he was watching movies before he was born. Not that such an assertion would have fazed the Dungannon people. I remember visiting Josie Woods in company with my mother, and when Josie had finished regaling us with some tale of long ago her young son John piped up, "Was I there Mummy?"

"Not at all, darling," responded Josie immediately. "You were up in Heaven driving a jeep for Baby Jesus."

The cinemas usually presented three shows a week, or if the film was a blockbuster, it might run for a whole week. There were no showings on Sunday. You got good value for your money, for you got the cartoons, the Movietone or Pathé news, the *Common Tractions* or trailers (work it out for yourself!), the wee picture, sometimes a short from British cinema, and the big picture, nearly always from Hollywood.

The Pathé news was introduced and concluded by the image of a crowing cockerel. A new arrival turned up in my dad's digs in Birmingham, in the shape of a young Irishman, and, noticing him moping about the house, my dad suggested he go to the pictures, there being a cinema just down the road. Later that evening my dad met him in the hall and asked if he had enjoyed himself.

"To be honest, now, I didn't think much of it," he confided.

Daddy was surprised, for that week's offering was reputed to be a good one. Then it occurred to him that perhaps the programme had changed.

"What was on?" he asked.

"I don't know what it was called," said the young fellow, "but an oul' cock come out and crowed, and there was a lot of people talking, and then the oul' thing come out and crowed again. A waste of me tanner, for all of ten minutes."

My dad's friend Bill Lynch loved the movies, laughingly referring to them as 'shadows on a sheet'. He always kept his cap on, no matter where he was, inside or out, and during one showing there were two ladies behind him who carried on a whispered conversation throughout the evening. Finally one said to the other in an audible hiss,

"If that man in front would take his cap off, we could see more."

"And if you two oul' biddies would stop chittering," Bill snapped back at them, "the man in the cap could hear more."

There were usually two showings or 'houses' in Dungannon, and if you were lucky you could go in for the first and stay on for the second, if there wasn't a big crowd. Not everybody wanted to do that except for the dedicated fans, but as someone who has seen *Calamity Jane* seven times, I can vouch for its having happened. There was frequently a queue for the new films, and it often went around the corner to Laverty's or Minnie Finnegan's, where they had long wooden counters with lift-up flaps, and sold sweets out of big glass jars. The ice cream that they sold in little flat tubs inside the cinema was as hard as the hobs of hell, but it tasted wonderful.

My family had a happy knack of making fun out of anything, or nothing. When, after my grandmother died, my cousin Mo stayed with us for a few months, she couldn't get a job because in those days you needed a work permit if you weren't born in Northern Ireland, but eventually she went to work in a shop owned by a friend of my mother's, Violet McCrory. McCrory's shop intrigued me, because it was actually two in one. If you selected the door to your left as you entered the narrow hallway from the street with its beautiful Victorian tiled floor, you found yourself in the tobacconist section, but if you turned right, you were in the Fancy Goods department, and for my eight-year-old self it was an Aladdin's cave, made even more magical by the fact that if you walked the length of the shop you would find yourself in the living quarters, which seemed to me very exotic. Occasionally mum would call with Violet for tea as she walked me home from school, and it was here that I first saw a tin of biscuits, for ours came packed into bags after being selected from large display cases in Madden's, later Kelly's, of Anne Street. It was Madden's that sold, when Mona was at school, bagfuls of broken biscuits for a penny. These were a good investment, for while you might get lots of plain ones, there was sure to be an iced one or a cream one in there too. On flush days she and her pals would go into old Mrs. Kelly's for a slider, and Mona often reflected on this good woman's generosity, and wonder how she could possibly have made any profit. No matter how many kids there were in the company, they all got a slider, even if only one or two of them had the money to pay for it. "Och, that wee girl could take an ice cream too."

Mo used to come home from work on a Saturday night laden with goodies: fish and chips, a real treat, though old Sarah Deakin used to dismiss them as 'a drunken man's supper'; a bottle of Shloer, which the others tolerated because I liked it, thinking it one step down from wine and therefore most glamorous; and a box of Turkish cigarettes, tiny little cylinders in a flip-top case, each wrapped in a different coloured paper – pink, green, blue, yellow, mauve. I was allowed to hold one of these as if I was smoking too, and very grown-up I felt. We'd pull the table into the centre of the floor in the basement kitchen in front of a huge fire, and dine like kings, with the lights out and only candlelight for illumination. Sometimes Mona would make rissoles, with floury potatoes and freshly minced steak from Donnelly's of Irish Street. If I was lucky I got to go shopping with mum for the meat, watching in fascination as the slabs of steak went into the mincer whole and came out in neat little swirls. I remember the big scrubbed wooden counters and the sawdust on the floor, and even as a child knew it was one of the cleanest butcher's shops I'd ever seen. The story is told that when the American soldiers first landed in Dungannon during the war, a member of the catering corps was dispatched to find suppliers of victuals, and he approached Francie Donnelly with a request to supply meat to the camp. This would have been a lucrative contract, and Francie was happy to oblige, but when he was told that they would want only his best meat, Francie replied that he would do what he could, but his best meat was always for his regular customers. I don't know if it's true or not, but I could well believe it. Somehow I can't see that happening in the big supermarkets of today.

I remember the first television set coming into the house when I was about five, a great chunk of bakelite with a built-in radio, but we never much cared for it. We used to have a wind-up gramophone, but Mona always wound it too tightly and broke the spring, and Wilf was always threatening not to fix it. We read copiously – poetry of all kinds, romance from Ethel M Dell and Margaret Pedlar, some of the classics, the Brontës and *Lorna Doone* being among our favourites, and *True Detective* magazine. To the day she died, mum loved true crime books, and I used to tease her that she was plotting the perfect murder. My dad sent me *Classics Illustrated* from Dublin, and I spent my pocket money on books from Miss Todd's shop in Scotch Street. This was another long narrow shop with a tall glass-fronted cabinet on one side filled with marvellous titles: *Front-Page Anne Thorne,* about a girl reporter; *Worrals Down Under,* from the creator of Biggles; *Shirley Flight, Air Hostess; Pomeroy's Postscript; Lion's Crouch; Stolen Holiday;* all rattling good reads stylishly presented in hardback with proper dust-jackets. She used to supply the High School with books for prize-givings, beautiful large format volumes, lavishly illustrated, and these she kept upstairs away from the hoi-polloi. When she found out that I was a bookworm, I was given my pick of them. I still have two, which I treasure: an animal encyclopaedia, and a large book of folk tales from around the world.

Mona read more widely than any of us, and if she got a bee in her bonnet about something she would pursue it like a diligent grub going through an apple. She loved Tennyson's *The Charge of the Light Brigade,* as I did, but while I was happy with the account in the poem, she read exhaustively about the Crimean war, military tactics past and present, and the life and career of Lord Cardigan.

This love of reading almost got her into trouble, though the situation was not of her making. One of our dearest friends was Annie Convery, who, as Miss Hamill, had taught Mona in the Convent primary school. Lawrence's book *Lady Chatterley's Lover* was then very much in the news and someone had loaned Annie a copy. She was having a sneak peek at it in class while the children were engaged in some written exercise, when the door opened to admit the Reverend Mother. Annie really didn't want to discuss her choice of literature with her, so quick as a flash she leant across and set the book onto the desk immediately below her, which was occupied by the young Mona. The nun completed her business and turned to go. At the last minute she stepped back and remarked,

"Let's see what wee Mona is reading now!"

Wee Mona was too small to say anything, but of course Annie had to confess, not only to ownership of the book but to the act of having, as it were, used Mona as a decoy. Many a laugh we shared about the incident in later years.

It was Annie who was buttonholed by a fellow traveller on a bus to Knock, with the whispered communication,

"Did you notice that thon woman has three busts at the back?"

Annie was, by her own account, agog to catch a glimpse of this marvel of nature, but the sight eluded her, despite her companion's attempts to identify her quarry. Later in the day her informant caught Annie's attention as they walked along, and pointed out a woman directly in front. Only then did Annie realise that the seam of the woman's coat had ripped, and was gaping in three places.

One of our favourite pastimes was dancing Irish jigs in the kitchen with mum providing the music by lilting. She was following a fine tradition, for it wasn't uncommon at ceilidhs years ago, if there wasn't a handy musician, or if he had succumbed to too much *uisce beatha,* to get some old fellow to provide gob-music; in Passage, they called it puss-music. We were once threatened with a visit from an acquaintance we didn't particularly want to see, and God forgive us, we decided not to answer the door when she called. She knocked two or three times, but we remained silent and watchful like The Listeners in Walter de la Mare's poem, the youngsters dying to giggle and mum with finger on lips shushing us, but also dying to giggle. Probably only Aunt Mona had the decency to feel bad. Finally our caller took herself off. We were thrilled, and having put the kettle on for the celebratory cup of tea, mum began to lilt *The Irish Washerwoman* or *The Rakes of Mallow* in her fine contralto, and soon it was round the house and mind the dresser, ceilidh swings and all! Several minutes later, a movement at the window caught my eye, and there was our visitor staring in at us with a horrified expression on her face as if she had just caught us in the act of dismembering a body. We had forgotten the back door. We were too breathless with dancing and laughing to do anything other than stare back at her, but it didn't really matter. As soon as she had collected her scattered wits she was off down the garden path at a trot to rejoin a saner society elsewhere.

The fact that there was access round the back to our house was both a blessing and a curse. It was a tall Edwardian house, two storeys high where it fronted onto the Donaghmore Road, and three at the back because of the basement kitchen. Like the other neighbours we spent most of our time below stairs, and close friends knew if they knocked and got no answer at the front door, there was always the tradesman's entrance if they were keen enough, or if their errand was important. We liked this arrangement, but it had its drawbacks.

One night we were settling down for a good read, when Mo appeared, dressed in only her bra and skirt, for she had been washing her hair. She had a towel wrapped round her head, and was about to shake out her thick dark mane to dry it when the door knocked. We knew at once that it was Doctor Who[12], a peculiar fellow who numbered our house among his ports of call and on this occasion I have to admit that we were not in the mood!

"Don't open the door till I get clothes on!" shrieked Mo with laudable presence of mind.

"It's only Doctor Who," said mum, "we'll not bother. Anyway, he'll come back later." It wasn't uncommon for the Doctor to arrive for his ceilidh at midnight.

"He'll go round the back," opined Mona, realising he knew the form. We therefore switched off the light in the kitchen, determined to play possum, while he continued the barrage of knocking with great application, no doubt mindful of his experience at Poker's house.

The light extinguished, the curtains drawn, we settled down to wait, but there was a glorious fire blazing in the grate, for if there was one thing the Campbells all liked it was a good fire. There was precious little we could do about that, but recognising that if the Doctor went round the back he would see the glare and know that we were in, we huddled around it to conceal the glow. The giggles began, sparked off by my mother's wry observation that we were like three tramps round a ha'penny candle, even though there were four of us, and by her recounting the story of Hughie Heyburn, welcoming visitors to his father's wake.

"I'm sorry for your trouble." The oft-repeated phrase was getting plenty of use that night. "Your father was a good man, God rest him."

"Aye, he was," agreed Hughie, in all innocence. "He loved a bit of crack, and he loved a good fire. I hope that wherever he is the night he has a good fire, and that he'll have it eternally."

We tensed as a footstep approached from the rear. There was a moment's silence, the sound of feet on gravel, then… the back door opened and in walked the Doctor while we stared at him like rabbits caught in headlamps, and then at one another, each

---

12 Doctor Who was the nickname given to Gerald

asking the silent question, "Did nobody think to lock the back door?" I can see him still, the firelight glinting off the lenses of his glasses as he gazed down on the four of us hunched, stupefied, on the hearth, our mouths open catching flies, staring at him as if he had indeed just recently exited the Tardis.

"Maureen, Mona, Aideen, Maureen, you appear to be in the dark. Is something wrong?" He always addressed each person in the room by name, like Yeats, numbering them out in a verse.

My mother's first instinct was to blame a blown light bulb but then good sense reminded her that we would have replaced it, so she mumbled something about a power failure, while young Maureen – Mo – fled in confusion with the towel strategically dropped from her hair to her shoulders.

"Strange," pursued the Doctor, "yours seems to be the only house affected. Every other house on the street is displaying a light."

We were forced to remain in the dark and allow a decent interval to elapse before 'trying' the lights to see if the power was back on, and exclaiming in delighted surprise when the simple flick of a switch flooded the room with illumination.

"The oul' carn," I heard my mum mutter later. "Bad enough catching us out, without rubbing our noses in it. Not that we didn't deserve it."

When we weren't hiding from the Doctor, crosswords were a favourite pastime, a passion shared by Patsy Bloomfield, a lifelong friend who was with my mother in the Musical Society. Years later they had not lost their taste for conundrums, and I would often answer the phone to hear Patsy's unmistakable voice, a smoky, husky, lived-in voice, always on the edge of a laugh.

"Have them two oul' bitches finished The Stinker? What did they get for ten across?"

She visited us for years, leaving the house at all hours of the morning. As the Troubles took hold, mum used to make Daddy sit up so he could walk her home. Since she would often stay till

three, and he got up at six-thirty, Patsy eventually issued an ulti-
matum: either he would go on to bed and she would walk home
alone, or she would stop coming. She was a tough cookie. He
went to bed.

She was a natural on the stage, doing a stint with the inimita-
ble James Young in the Group Theatre, and she graced many an
amateur production before and since. I saw her once in John B.
Keane's *The Field*. I think she spoke a couple of sentences and
was required to contribute a few gusts of laughter, and that was
it. She stole the show. As a wise adjudicator once told us during
the Mid-Ulster Festival of Amateur Drama in Carrickmore, there
are no small parts, only small actors. She even tackled drama in
Irish, though she was not an Irish speaker, and would get Art
McCaughey to tutor her on pronunciation. She left our house
one morning as the stars paled and the dawn chorus was starting up. She was carrying a straw basket containing a bottle of
potín that someone had given her, two blessed candles that she
was to deliver to the hospital, the script of a play in Irish, and an
umbrella. Mum always watched her to the top of Anne Street,
and she saw her being stopped by an army foot patrol yards from
our door.

"Good morning, madam."

"Morning, son."

"Do you mind if I look in you basket, madam?"

"Not at all, son."

He passed over the bottle and the candles with a wary look,
then unrolled the script.

"Do you mind if I have a look at this document, madam?"
Patsy chuckled.

"Not one bit, son, but if you can read that, you're a better man
than I am, Gunga Din!"

As he handed back her belongings and stood aside to let her
pass, she produced the umbrella. With a smile she resumed her
progress along the street, singing *The Sash,* and beating time on
the lamp posts with the gamp.

She asked us once if she could come and spend the evening of Christmas day with us.

"Of course," we assured her. "You'll be very welcome." And we meant it.

"Are you sure?" she pursued. "I mean, you won't have family or anyone else to visit, will you?"

To convince her of her welcome, Mona insisted,

"Not at all. Sure who would come out of their own house on a Christmas night?"

Fortunately, this was Patsy, who would often arrive unannounced and greet you at the door with, "The two oul' bitches don't want me but I'm comin' in anyway."

She was always wanted in our house.

The Dead and the Undead

Aideen at Trinity, 1974

"But did you ever see a ghost?"

A winter's day, three of them hunkered round the fire in the room behind the Salon in Hanover Square, Coagh, taking a break from dressing hair: my mother, her pal and colleague, Freddie, and their young apprentice Lily, along with their boss, Mrs. Agnew, and Mrs. Agnew's brother, one of five who had gone into the service of the Church, home for a holiday.

Why is it that we always assume ministers of religion are more likely to have had a brush with the supernatural than ordinary folk? Is it that we think them more in tune with an other reality? Or is it that we push at the boundaries of possibility with those who might be expected to have thought about it, looking for confirmation – or denial – to allay our own fears or confirm our beliefs? Who knows? Not the girls gathered round that fire, on that day, of that I'm certain. Father Pat looked thoughtful. "I'm not sure," he admitted. This was good; there was a story here. "I was stationed in Bridlington during the War," he began, "and I had had a very busy few days. I staggered home one night, utterly exhausted, and told my housekeeper, an Irishwoman called Mary, that I was going straight to bed, and she was not to disturb me on any account, unless it be a sick call." He looked into the flames, remembering.

"I barely had my head on the pillow when I heard a knock at the door, subdued voices, and with a sinking feeling, I heard Mary begin the ascent of the stairs. She scratched at the door. 'I'm sorry, Father, but there's someone very ill…'

"I said it was all right and climbed back into my clothes. When I got downstairs there was a man waiting for me in the hall. He was very dark, with a shock of coal-black hair and a thick beard obscuring most of his face, and I knew a moment's hesitation. This was during the blackout, and he was a stranger to me. He saw my uncertainty. 'There's a man who needs you, Father.'

"'That's fine,' I agreed, putting on a coat. 'Who is it?' for I assumed it would be one of my parishioners.

"'No one you know,' he told me. 'He's a crewman on a ship. I'll take you to him.'

"My heart sank again, for the docks area was a rough place at the best of times, and in the middle of a blackout, in wartime… no matter, if there was a soul in need of assistance, I would have to go. We headed off into the night and my companion spoke not a word, only guiding me with absolute certainty until we came to the docks. He led me up to a ship and said, 'This is where he is,' then he turned and left me.

"I stood for a few minutes irresolute, not knowing what to do next, but eventually I hailed a man and told him of my errand. He knew of no one who might have sent the call, but he took me to the Captain, where I explained, feeling somewhat foolish, that I had been summoned to attend a sick man, whose name I didn't even know. I described the messenger, assuming that he at least would be known, but the Captain told me there was no one answering that description among his crew, and we agreed that a man of so singular appearance could not easily be overlooked. The Captain might have seen me off for a mad cleric but he treated me with great courtesy, and said I might go anywhere on the ship to find the man, though he had no knowledge of any of his crew *in extremis* either. He assigned a young seaman to help me and we searched the ship. We found him eventually, a man in a fever, huddled in a tiny cabin somewhere in the bowels of the ship, and my young companion left us together. I knew nothing of the man's history, but I saw at once that the last thing that man wanted was a priest! He insulted me in every way possible, with curses and obscenities, told me I had no business there, but as he went in and out of delirium I began to sense a desire in him for more normal communication that he was fighting, or the devil was fighting, so I fought too!"

Father Pat paused, and looked at his audience. "Do any of you know that Service poem about Salvation Bill?" My mum did, and smiled, knowing what was coming.

"And then and there, with plea and prayer, I wrestled for his soul," Father Pat paraphrased softly. "It was just like that, and a hard struggle I had, for he had turned his back on religion many years before. But eventually he made his confession to me, thank God. I gave him absolution, and afterwards I gave him the Last Rites, for he was very weak. I sat with him for a while and he slept; and when he woke, much calmer, he thanked me.

"'How did you know I was sick, Father?' he wanted to know. I stared at him, baffled. 'But you sent for me.' The man laughed, a little bit of the hysteria returning.

"'Not I! Do you think the man I was when you walked in here would have called for a priest?'

"It seemed unlikely, but I described my visitor and the man denied all knowledge of him. I thought perhaps he was still not quite lucid, so I took my leave. As I came down the gangway of the ship, wondering how I would get home, my dark-avised companion rejoined me. 'All well, Father?'

"'All's well,' I confirmed. Of course I was dying to ask the question, but something held me back. 'I'll wait till we're nearer home, I thought,' still half afraid, no, more than half afraid. But when we got to my front door my companion was gone, just gone, not in any dramatic manner, nothing like that, he just wasn't there. I fell into bed shattered, and didn't wake till well into the following afternoon."

The girls were agog. "So who was it? What was it?"

"I don't know," he told them honestly. "That's my experience, exactly as it happened to me, and I am no wiser than you. Perhaps someone at home was praying for the man, a mother, a sister, who knows? And I thought afterwards my strange visitor might have been St. Joseph, patron of a happy death. Who can say?"

Who indeed? What do any of us know of death? We all experience it, we all have to go through it, and we none of us understand anything at all about it.

They say a violent death leaves an impression behind, a twitch upon the thread of time that reverberates down the years so that it can be felt at a distance. My mother was in Kathleen's shop one night when a young man burst in white-faced and shaking. "Does anyone know Teddy McCall?" he enquired, looking wildly about him.

"Yes," said Kathleen, "Teddy lives on down the street a bit," and she gave directions.

The man went out but was back in seconds. "Look," he said, "my mate in the car is in a bad way, I don't think he'll make it any further. Can I bring him in?"

He returned with another companion who looked just as deathly as he did, supporting a third young man between them, whom they settled down in the kitchen behind the shop. He was in a state of nervous collapse, and could barely speak, his eyes rolling and unfocused, his breathing shallow and laboured. Teddy was sent for and recognised the young man at once, but though he tried to get sense out of him with the help of a wee drop of brandy and strong tea, there was no improvement. They debated calling a doctor, but finally he asked for a priest, and a call went down to the Parochial house. While they were waiting for someone to come, my mum said to his two companions,

———— ∞ ————

"What in under God happened to you?" They were, as they say, stone cold sober, seemed reasonable young men, and it was clearly not a prank.

"I'll tell you as far as I know," said the one who had first appeared, explaining that they were not local, but had been coming from a football match in Coalisland. "Jack was driving. We were chatting away about the game, and just as we reached the Flourmill Bridge, Jack threw up his hands and shouted, "Oh, Jesus Christ!" and covered his face. The car went into a spin and I grabbed the wheel and got her righted, but we could have been killed. I got her stopped and we got Jack out, but could get no sense out of him. We thought he'd had some kind of seizure, but finally he mentioned Teddy's name and where he lived, and we didn't know what else to do, so we came here."

His audience was as puzzled as he was, but at that point Fr. McGarvey arrived and was shown in to the kitchen, where he was left alone with the stricken Jack. Conversation was desultory, no one knowing what to say, whether they should try to behave as if nothing had happened and talk about the weather. After a while, Fr. McGarvey emerged.

"He'll be all right," he told them, "he's had a shock, but he'll be fine. Get him home now, and I want all of you to promise faithfully that you won't ask him what happened. He'll tell you in his own good time, just don't hassle him."

The promise was given willingly enough but with many a raised eyebrow and exchange of glances. Mum was dying to know the details but nothing was said as a much calmer and slightly embarrassed young man was put back into the car and driven away.

Several weeks passed and then Teddy hailed my mother as she crossed the street. "Maureen, do you mind yer man who came looking for me that night after the football match?"

"I do well," she said.

"And do you mind Cecil Davison?"

She did, and so did most of the people in Dungannon, for Cecil's fast and reckless driving was legendary, and even in the days when there were fewer cars on the road, he was reckoned to be a danger to himself and anything he might meet. Finally everyone's dire prophecies were proved true, for one night as he was coming home from Coalisland, he hit a bus at the Flourmill Bridge at speed, and was killed outright. Teddy's young friend did not know Cecil, did not know of the accident, possibly didn't even know the name of the bridge, but as he approached it he had seen the accident re-enacted before his eyes in every detail, so vividly that he thought himself caught up in it. Whether he was more frightened to discover that he had just witnessed an illusion – an echo – a shadow on the page of history – rather than an episode happening in real time, is anyone's guess.

When my mother had her own salon on the Donaghmore Road, one of her most regular clients was Mrs. Loy, whose family owned a pub in Anne Street. She had glorious auburn hair, and all it ever needed was a wash and trim. My mother loved working with it as much as she enjoyed its owner's company. One day it occurred to mum that she hadn't seen Mrs. Loy for weeks, and speculated that she might be ill. After a few more weeks had gone by, she began to worry that she might have inadvertently given offence, for such an interval between visits was unusual. Then she had a call from Peggy, a close friend of Mrs. Loy's, saying that she wanted to explain her absence. This is her story.

Loy's pub was only a stone's throw from the market yard, and was a favourite retreat when the buying and selling were done on a Tuesday and a Thursday. The dealin' men from Crossmaglen might have put whiskey in the tay, but in Dungannon, they took their tipple in Loy's. A regular caller was Bob, who would stand at the end of the bar, sink a few pints, and enjoy the crack, so he was much mourned when he passed away quite suddenly, and many a one would remark that you would miss him from his accustomed post. One night, many weeks after Bob's demise and well after the pub had been closed up and everyone sent on their homeward way, Mrs. Loy was on her way to bed when she heard a noise from the public bar, where no one had any right to be. She went to investigate, switching on the light as she entered. There in his usual place stood Bob, seemingly as solid and strong as he had been in life, and it was fully thirty seconds before she realised that what she was seeing was not possible, and she felt her blood run cold. She ran out of the bar and up to her bedroom, tucking herself into bed and telling herself not to be foolish, but she was seriously frightened, and in the morning she woke to find handfuls of her gorgeous hair on the pillow. It continued to fall out over the following weeks so that she had to wear a scarf, and though eventually it grew back, it grew white, and never regained its former lustre.

In 1974 in Dublin, many people met an untimely end when a series of car bombs exploded across the city. When I was debating what to do after school, the Troubles were at their height, and my mother was terrified of my going to Belfast. I wasn't keen on the prospect myself, so my dad's suggestion of Trinity met with general approval. Ironically, I have never been as near to a bomb in all my time in Northern Ireland as I was that day in Dublin, for one of the booby-trapped cars was parked right at the back of the college grounds in Lincoln Place, beside the gateway I was planning to walk through. It was tea time. I was in the grill bar gathering my bits together when a friend of mine came in. We chatted for a few minutes, thus briefly delaying my departure, then I took my leave. I was going via the back gate because Dublin was in the throes of a city bus strike and I had arranged to get a lift there. As I walked across the podium of the Berkeley Library, a fireball erupted fifty yards in front of me, right at my proposed point of exit. The next few hours were filled with pandemonium and horror, but eventually we got back to our lodgings, and I tried to phone home to say I was safe. But the telephone system was jiggered, with some lines down and others jammed, and mobiles hadn't been invented. I knew my mother would be up the walls but there was nothing anyone could do. It would be another twenty-four hours before things were even halfway back to normal.

The following day a friend of mine took the provincial bus home to Dungannon. Arrived in The Square, she went looking for a taxi to bring her the extra two or three miles home. She got Raymond Quinn – Raymond, our taxi man for many a year, married to Kathleen, who kept the shop at the top of our street. Good-natured, chatty, and genuinely interested in his fares, he talked away to Maryan, and soon established that she was recently arrived from Dublin, where she was a student. Of course they spoke of the bombs the day before. Having no phone in the house, we, like most of the neighbours, used the one at the back of Kathleen's shop, so he was well aware of the agonies my mother had been going through in trying to reach me. "Do you know Aideen D'Arcy?" he hazarded.

"I do indeed," replied Maryan. She might have added that we had been at school together.

"You wouldn't happen to know if she's all right, with them bombs and all?"

"Actually, I do," replied Maryan. "I met her coming across Front Square yesterday evening."

"After the bombs went off?" He was taking no chances.

"Yes."

"You're sure it was after the bomb?"

"Positive."

He couldn't get her dropped off quickly enough, and as soon as he got back to his own house, he broke the good news to Kathleen, who dispatched Raymond junior, all of about nine or ten, I guess, with instructions to inform my mother that I had been spotted after the tragedy, and was safe and well. Charged with such important tidings, and eager to give them the solemnity they deserved, the young Mercury delivered his salvo with great gusto as my mother opened the front door. "Mrs. D'Arcy! Me ma says to tell you that your Aideen's not dead!"

Blind Horses and Wet Grass

Maureen Campbell D'Arcy
– storyteller extraordinaire

My mum didn't like a barefooted cup of tea so I'd often be sent to the shop for 'some small bread' to accompany the many drops that she needed to sustain her throughout the day. As blood is to a vampire, so is tea to a Campbell, and I feel physically ill if I don't get my afternoon fix. Small bread meant nothing too sweet, but not a sliced pan; maybe a donkey's nose, or a sinker, or a Veda loaf. She detested fresh bread and preferred to let a loaf sit for two days before she'd eat it, so we needed to stockpile.

She was a dab hand at persuading some of us to make the tea for her, usually by dropping a broad hint or rolling her eyes towards the cooker with a hungry look. All our dogs copied it from her. She had another method she employed with Mona.

My aunt was one of the fussiest women I ever knew, to the point where she drove the rest of us mad, but we got used to

———— ❧ ————

her asking the inevitable question, "Have you washed your hands?" before you even entered the kitchen, let alone tried to cook anything. She rinsed pots every time before she used them, even though she was the one who did the washing-up, and once cleaned a mirror so thoroughly that she took the silver off the back. It might have been this mirror that occasioned one of her famous Mona-isms, a turn of phrase so odd, yet so apt, that it had us all in stitches. Someone asked her if she had been a bit off-colour recently for she wasn't looking her best. Had she lost weight?

"I don't know about that," she replied, "but this morning I went to wipe a smear off the mirror and then realised it was my own reflection."

It might have been the same day she searched through the hot press for a particular towel and couldn't find it, but when I went to look I came across it in no time.

"Imagine that!" she was amazed. "And I thought I didn't see it."

When mum wanted to encourage Mona to make the tea, it was a case of:

"Mona, do you want a drop of tea?"

"Have you washed your hands?"

"No."

"I'll make it."

But mum was also adept at avoiding taking a hint if she so chose, on the numerous occasions when we tried her own tactics to get her to do something for us! Her reply was always the same.

"I know what you mean, but the grass is wet." And that was that.

Like all the sayings adopted by the Campbells down the years, the whole family used this one willy-nilly without giving much thought to its origins. It simply meant that though the hearer knew precisely what you were getting at, he or she wasn't prepared to bite. It was employed in all sorts of circumstances, and was not confined to the making of tea. It was, in essence, a saying capable of universal application. There were many such phrases that peppered our everyday speech, many of them truncated or skewed to meet a particular situation. If you told Mona an unlikely story she would favour you with a sidelong look laced with incredulity and say,

"Now, that's as I rode out."

This was short for *as I rode out and forgot to come back,* and there are not many more unlikely excuses than that one!

If she was engaged in a dispute with you and it was clear that there was going to be a stalemate, Mona never lost her temper, but accepted that there is usually room for more than one point of view at a time. "You away, then," she'd say; more shorthand, for *you away and I'll go round,* or you go your way and I'll go mine.

If you were promised something that she thought was unlikely to materialise, she would say with a knowing nod, "Aye, live, horse!" being an abbreviation of *live horse and you'll eat grass;* an empty promise.

"You're looking quare and well, Maureen," someone would say.

"At a distance," she'd reply, no doubt inspired by Mrs. Quinn of cobweb fame, whose reply to the same compliment was, "At a distance, like a frog on a tether."

One of the phrases I most associate with my mum was the response she gave when she was offered more tea or a second helping of something:

"Thank you, no. I have enjoyed an elegant sufficiency of enoughness."

An elegant sufficiency accounted for many a measure in our house. And on second thoughts, she would have accepted the tea.

This tendency of ours to collect words and phrases as a kind of private argot gave us many a laugh, but could cause embarrassment when you forgot that not everybody was tuned in to your wavelength. This happened to Hugh Convery, a dear friend, who shared our love of language, its vagaries, and above all, its misuses. When his girls were small he used to mispronounce words deliberately for their amusement, and he always referred to the bollards in the middle of traffic islands as 'boulevards'.

"I knew it was time to stop," he told us in his dryly humorous tone, his bespectacled face alight with the fun of it, "when a motorist asked me for directions and I told him to go down the road and turn right at that boulevard…" We never called them anything else afterwards.

It was fashionable a few years ago for all and sundry to claim Irish descent, but it is my humble opinion that the famed Mrs. Malaprop could justly claim to have spawned more than a few progeny in Dungannon. Half the town was on infidelity benefit. Amy's daughter in Canada had a fernando around her house while another had a midget of a camera (you need to say it quickly!). The army travelled the roads in sarsfield trucks, while Mrs. Grimason had a pain in her abodement; another neighbour had her wound removed. Yet these people were neither ignorant nor stupid. They just had a way with the Queen's English that the Queen would find hard to cope with.

In school there were occasions when the teachers must have despaired of us, especially when it came to learning prayers, for there were those who simply tuned in to what others were saying – or seemed to be saying – without any thought for sense or meaning. In my class we had a girl who insisted upon saying *Hail Mary full of grace the Lord is a flea,* and another who belted out one of the great precepts of the Creed as *I believe in Jesus Christ who… suffered under a bunch of violets.* When Uncle Wilf was rehearsing his First Communion doctrine he had a prayer which referred to *Our Saviour who died like a criminal on the cross,* but Wilf could never be persuaded to say anything other than *died like a cripple on the cross.* I'm sure the good Lord knew we meant well.

Songsters too could get things wrong, and this drove my family crazy, even if it sometimes made us laugh. It was one of the reasons we regarded Makem and Clancy with near-reverence, for whatever come-all-ye they sang, in whatever version, the words always made sense. They would none of them have approved of the man who sang about a partridge in a fir tree, or murdered a sentimental ditty by singing *farewell my love, upon the dew.* We were treated to a rendition of *The Croppy Boy* at a party in a neighbour's house, in which the minstrel was so fired up, according to mum, that the veins were standing out on his forehead like chicken's biceps. When he came to the description of the villainous Captain who spoke *with fiery glare and with fury hoarse,* he spat out, *with fiery glare, and with curious host...* But perhaps the worst offence was committed by the man who couldn't get his head around the lines, *Where the thrush and the robin their sweet notes entwine, On the banks of the Suir that flows down by Mooncoin.* It didn't have quite the same ring when he sang *where the thrush ate the robin and two balls of twine...*

My mother's cousin Hugh McNichol had his own way with language. He came home in the trap from Magherafelt one evening and called his servant boy to put the outfit away.

"Extricate the quadruped from the vehicle," he instructed him, "and stabulate it; and I will reward you with a pecuniary compensation before the illuminator goes down beyond the horizon."

Daddy's favourite was this one, but I can't account for its provenance:

"A slight but rapid inclination of the cranium is as equivalent as a spasmodic movement of the outer membrane of the optic, to an equine quadruped devoid of its visual faculties." No, you figure it out! I had to. And here's another one he was fond of catching me and my friends with, slightly different in style but still a linguistic gem. Watch out for those all-important apostrophes! *If Moses was the son of Pharaoh's daughter, was he also the daughter of Pharaoh's son?* And no, you cannot argue that he was only a foster-son; it doesn't matter. Lynne Truss, eat your heart out!

Sayings come and sayings go, but *I know what you mean, but the grass is wet* remained a favourite for years. One day when I was about fifteen, I suddenly realised how odd it was, how apparently meaningless. Just as sometimes you look at a person or an object and see them in a completely different light, so now I enunciated this often-used phrase and heard it, as it were, for the first time.

"Mum?"

"Yes?"

"What does that actually mean? You know, where does it come from? It's really peculiar."

"Would it help if I told you the rest of it?" she asked, a distinct twinkle in her eye, always a bad sign! Mrs. Agnew told the apprentices in Coagh to 'watch out for Miss Campbell when her eyes start to shine!' But this time, it was only with merriment.

"It might," I told her, "but I didn't know there was any more to it."

She grinned.

"Och, 'deed there is. It goes like this: *I know what you mean, but the grass is wet, and tuppence is too little. Produce the chocolate first!* Now do you see?"

I did, I do; and that's how I like to remember her, eyes brimming with devilment, loving to surprise you. She could reduce you to hysterics with a lift of her brows, a shrug of the shoulder, a twist of a song. She could make you so mad you'd cheerfully have strangled her, and the next minute turn your tears of anger or frustration to tears of helpless laughter. After her death, most of the letters of condolence focused on the same attributes: her sense of fun, her humour, her love of conversation, her good nature; these gifts she shared liberally with all the marvellous people who populated my childhood country. And she was a Campbell. She could always laugh at herself.

Wherever she is today, I hope she's still laughing.

I hope she knows that I am too.

Mamma Mia

We were close when I was younger,
My mother and I.

She knew how to tell stories,
Wear a turban, sing a song.

Her friends loved her.

She could peel an apple in one piece,
Throw it over my shoulder and divine
The name of my future husband
From the way it fell.

We were close as I grew up,
My mother and I.

She loved fashion,
Adored shoes,
Liked mini-skirts,
And smoked.

My friends loved her.

We fell out as I grew older,
My mother and I.

She learned how to worry,
Foresaw disaster in every outing
I took or planned.
She grew selfish, wanted to come with me.

I wanted to live my life.
So did she.

My boyfriends loved her.

We fought a war of attrition,
My mother and I.

They say we're alike now, her friends and mine:
I have her legs, her smile, her way of spinning yarns,
Her bad laugh.

We came close as she grew older,
My mother and I.
When she fought to the death,
And was not frightened,
And let me go.

The nurses loved her.

And today,
As I stood before the mirror to brush my hair,
We looked back at me from the glass, smiling:
My mother and I.

Snapshots

Aideen's great grandfather Sheeran (left), with her father, Patrick (front), brother Tom and friends. Second right is Johnny Morrissey, a native Irish speaker

Pat the dog-lover, with Buffy, a neighbour's puppy

*Congratulations card from Lil to
Patrick and Maureen when Aideen
was born – the coverlet in pink satin
was very smart in 1954!*

*Aunt Lil, who
came home to die*

*Patrick marching with the Forresters. He was never a member, but was per-
suaded to join to swell the ranks. Behind him is John Campbell, and in front,
his pal Seamus McKeown. Geordie Rocks is just behind Seamus's left shoulder.*

Pub quiz champions, c. 1986. Patrick D'Arcy second from right. On his right is team-mate Sean Campbell, one of 'Hawkeye's' sons.

Charlie McKenna, lifelong friend who kept a decent pub in Irish Street

A few of Charlie's regulars: l-r – Patrick, Charlie, Noel Madden, Tommy Rooney and Seamus McKeown

The family at Passage: l-r – Mai, Rose, Cis (Granny D'Arcy), a friend, and Lil

Patrick, Aideen and Granny D'Arcy

Aideen, on the strand at Passage, c. 1972

Grandmother D'Arcy's house in Passage

Grandfather D'Arcy

Great pals Bessie Rooney (left), Maureen and Bridie McKenna (Charlie's wife), with others, at a Parish social

Dear Reader

I hope you have enjoyed this publication from Ballyhay Books. It is one of a growing number of local interest books published under this imprint including *Lie Over Da,* also by Aideen D'Arcy, Hugh Robinson's books *Back Across the Fields of Yesterday, The Book of One Thousand Beautiful Things and Other Favourites* and *Yarns from the Ards,* John O'Sullivan's *Belfast City Hospital, a Photographic History,* Viv Gotto's *Footprints in the Sea, Songs of the County Down* by Jackie Boyce, Harry Allen's *Men of the Ards,* and *Roosters and Hens for the Appreciative Eye* by Suze Craig and Ros Harvey.

To see details of these books as well as the beautifully illustrated books of our sister imprint, Cottage Publications, why not visit our website at **www.cottage-publications.com** or contact us at:–

Laurel Cottage
15 Ballyhay Rd
Donaghadee
Co. Down
N. Ireland
BT21 0NG

Tel: +44 (0)28 9188 8033

Timothy & Johnson

BALLYHAY BOOKS